Thanks for dropp...

Good luck in the kitchen!

Buzzy

2019

Pants Off

salmon

Pants Off salmon

JoJo

PUBLISHING

Alec Bragg

About the author

I was raised in country NSW on a sheep and cattle property. Attending boarding school wasn't a great start to my culinary experiences, although in retrospect it showed me how to completely cook all the goodness from vegetables. I graduated from the University of Queensland as a physiotherapist and then, living in a share house, had to learn how to cook. Thankfully some previous lessons with a patient mother in the farm kitchen, followed by regular dinner sessions with an old chef mate meant I gradually learnt the basics and then a few more tricks to make it all easier.

Pants Off Salmon and Other Recipes for Bachelors was my first foray into the world of cookbook writing. It showed me that blokes really want to learn how to cook but are mostly too scared to do it. It also showed me that it wasn't only the bachelors who wanted to impress with their cooking, hence the revised version, *Pants Off Salmon — Recipes to Impress.*

I still work as a physiotherapist but now live on a farm in the Sunshine Coast hinterland. The plan is to continue cooking and writing, whilst running some cattle and growing some quality produce on the farm block.

Welcome one and all to *Pants Off Salmon 2nd Edition*

So much has happened in the twelve months since the first book was published, all of which has exceeded my expectations. So, thank you to everyone who bought the book, read one of my articles or watched a TV segment. (I'll get that pan hot enough next time, I promise!)

Originally, I designed these recipes because bachelors wanted a cookbook designed to help them knock the socks off their dates (as well as anything else) with their cooking skills. What I hadn't realised was how many bachelorettes, happy couples, and even the married crew were anxious to impress with their cooking, often joking about the pleasurable results they achieved. They wanted more. Where was their book, they demanded?

Well, here it is!

I've made some changes this time round. There are more recipes but I have stayed with the original principles of *Pants Off Salmon and Other Recipes for Bachelors*. The last thing I want to do is make cooking good meals difficult or stressful (and reducing you to tears). That's for TV cooking shows, not my book! After all, if I can pull these off without a hitch, not to mention formal cooking training, then anyone can.

I've also included desserts in this edition, as we all know that a good meal is even better when it is followed by a nice pudding! We all like our desserts! (Hint, hint.)

It is encouraging to hear that everyone likes to try to impress in his or her own kitchen. This book has been designed with that in mind — to help you do just that.

Some things though have been a huge hit. While the original panty-drop rating was received in the humorous, irreverent vein in which it was intended, I've decided to broaden the gender scope and now call it the 'pants drop rating' to indicate the recipes rating. So, watch out, all you wearers of boxer shorts! No one is safe now!

The wine suggestions were often the pivotal factor when used by avid readers cooking these recipes, so I've expanded on these wherever possible and extended it to include beer, when appropriate.

The etiquette section proved to be a godsend to struggling bachelors, many of whom claim they're no longer struggling as a result. So, look out for more new guidelines in that section.

Cooking doesn't have to be a chore. It can be downright fun, not to mention rewarding. With that in mind, I hope you'll roll up your sleeves and try out the recipes for yourself. (As always, pants are optional.)

I would like to extend a warm and sincere thanks to all of my friends and family, bachelors or not, who have generously contributed ideas for meals that have worked for them. I've enjoyed putting this together and I'm sure you'll enjoy taking this book out for a test drive down Lovers' Lane. So, till next time, enjoy!!

And as mother always said, "Wear your best underwear whenever you go out. You never know what might happen to you!"

Alec Bragg

Contents

Desserts

How to use this book

*P*ants Off Salmon 2nd Edition has been written to make cooking good quality, impressive meals easy enough for just about anybody.

Basic, step-by-step instructions are included and instructions have been listed in a way to ensure that everything comes together at the right time. Each recipe unless otherwise stated makes a serving for two people.

I have included preparation and cooking times to help you to better gauge when you should start cooking in relation to when your guest arrives, and, just as important, how much wine you'll need!

The pants drop rating is admittedly a somewhat novel guide to measure the potential success and impressiveness of each meal. Look out for the ⛛ ▨ which indicate the pants drop rating. That said, don't bother skimming through looking for the 5-drop rating, looking for a shoo-in (or guaranteed pants off, in this case), because there aren't any. There is no such thing as perfection! Thus, there are no meals here rated 5 out of 5. After all, I don't want any of you calling me to complain that your meal didn't get the desired result! Ratings are based on results and therefore are always subject to change. (Think of that financial products disclaimer: Past results are no guarantee of future performance.) With that in mind, once you've taken a few of these fired-up recipes for a spin, check out www.pantsoffsalmon. com, and let me know how you make out...so to speak!

Etiquette

When I first moved forward with this cooking guide, the subject of etiquette never even occurred to me. Yet, one evening I found myself sitting down to a meal with a good mate of mine who was really struggling to click with someone. He was willing to bring them home and cook for them, and he wasn't a bad cook by any means, but he couldn't figure out why he wasn't making any progress in the romance department. It dawned on me, as he took me through a typical date, what it was that he was doing all wrong.

Whether it was at home or in a restaurant, he would race through his meal, intent only on what he viewed as 'dessert'. He was sailing hard and fast towards where he envisioned the finish line to be (invariably upstairs). Every romantic outing inevitably became a shipwreck. Not surprisingly, the prize continually floated out of his reach.

I realised that my mate was far from unusual. If anyone else was behaving or doing the same things as he was, there were a lot of guys out there in need of a lifesaver.

With that in mind, here are a few pointers that have helped others:

- Pace yourself. Never *ever* finish your meal before your guest. Gauge their speed so that you finish at the same time. Try putting down your fork between bites if you're having trouble slowing down.
- Talk! Even more important, listen! Conversation is critical for people to feel comfortable with each other. Let your guest know that you are capable of and smart enough to hold a conversation, and that you care about what they have to say. If your guest is simply blowing smoke, well, take a few deep breaths and try not to cough.
- Turn off the electronics. That includes the television, your mobile phone, any and every form of computer, and even the ringer off your landline — anything that can potentially steer your attention away from your date. Stereo systems set to play soft music should

be the only exception to this rule. You may even score points if you ask your guest to turn off their phone as it lets them know you've turned off yours and are intent on only focusing on them. (And on not burning dinner, of course!)

- Don't try to encourage compliments on your cooking by taking the initiative and complimenting yourself. Just because your guest doesn't rave ecstatically and jump up and down in excitement doesn't mean they're not secretly wondering whether you might just turn out to be as fabulous as your food is.

- Take any compliments that do come your way graciously, with a smile and a simple thank you. Your quiet confidence will impress them. If your meal is great but your guest fails to notice, well, then maybe they're just not good enough for you! But that's no reason for you not to continue to be polite.

- Check with your guest well in advance whether there is anything they don't or can't eat before you start cooking. Even the best seafood risotto isn't a resounding success if your guest goes into anaphylactic shock in front of you.

- Find out if they have a favourite wine. Even if it's just a matter of red versus white, there is no better wine to set the scene than their favourite, and it can help you zero in on the perfect meal to serve with it. Wine suggestions are included throughout, partly for that reason. If their choice makes your blood run cold or has you suppressing your gag reflex, see if you can excite their interest in trying something new that you think they might like. "Well, if you like that, then I think I know a wine you might enjoy even more!" is usually effective.

- Set a proper table. Have a separate knife, fork, spoon, etc., for every dish that needs them. If you need a salad fork, include it. That includes butter knives, serving spoons and forks — anything you might need. Don't ask them to use their dinner fork for their dessert just to cut down on the washing up! Use side plates for bread. Don't forget the serviettes. Even better, use cloth napkins. Avoid anything in the middle of the table such as a centrepiece that blocks your view of each other. (Tall, slender candles are okay.) Tiny tea lights are an incredibly inexpensive yet romantic option that won't prevent you from seeing eye to eye.

- Serve water as well as wine — and drink some. At the very least, it will save you from getting completely smashed.

Helpful hints

Shortcuts and tips are a cook's best friend. Like, what is a good, basic salad dressing that you can whip up in just minutes? Or, how do you make quick gravy? Will olive oil cause a rash if used later as a massage oil? (Probably not, unless they're allergic.)

Basic measurement equivalents
1 cup = 250 ml
1 tablespoon (tbsp) = 15 ml = 3 teaspoons
1 teaspoon (tsp) = 5 ml

Basic salad dressing (can be doubled)
2–3 tbsp olive oil
1 tsp balsamic or good quality white wine vinegar
1 tsp lemon juice
salt and pepper to taste
Optional: 1 tsp seeded or Dijon mustard

Basic chicken gravy (prepared by boiling in a saucepan)
1 tsp chicken stock powder
3/4 cup water
1 tsp tomato sauce or apricot jam
1/4 cup white wine
1 tsp corn flour (mixed first with a tablespoon of cold water into a paste)

Which wine with which meal?

I've elected to focus on Australian and New Zealand wines here.

Chicken: Classic dry whites, including Sauvignon Blanc, Semillon/Sauvignon Blanc blends, and any style of Chardonnay

Seafood: Riesling (dry, not sweet), Sauvignon Blanc, Verdelho

Beef: Shiraz, Shiraz/Viognier, GSM (Grenache/Shiraz/Mourverdre), Merlot, Cabernet and Cabernet blends, Zinfandel

Lamb: Cabernet Sauvignon, Cabernet/Shiraz, Zinfandel

Pizza: Sangiovese, Cabernet/Merlot blends

Vegetarian: Anything!! And lots of it!

Asian: Pinot Gris, Shiraz Viognier and Gewürztraminer

How to avoid food poisoning

Food safety, particularly nowadays, is something we all should be aware of. After all, the last thing you need is a sick dinner guest — sort of wrecks the moment. (And a sick host isn't conducive, either!)

When cutting up raw meats, poultry, etc., use a separate cutting board than the one intended for cutting your vegetables and other items. Wash your hands and your knives immediately afterwards and do it carefully — a spritz of bleach or an antibacterial wipe will help kill germs. If you must use the same cutting board and knives, wash and cut all your fruits and veggies first, and *then* cut your meats. This will stop cross-contamination from the raw meat. Wooden cutting boards have been proven to be safer than plastic for raw meats because studies have shown that the enzymes in the wood help eliminate salmonella. A safe way to wash these boards after cutting meats is to wash normally and then rinse with boiling water from the kettle.

In the fridge, place raw products on the bottom shelf so that no drips fall onto other food products. Cover food before being placed in the fridge. Leftovers don't need to cool down before being put in the fridge; it's actually safer to refrigerate them right away or within an hour or so of serving.

If marinating raw meat and you wish to use the marinade later as part of the sauce, the marinade must be boiled for several minutes in order to ensure it is safe for consumption.

Pants Off Recipes

Salmon Fillet on Sweet Potato and Pumpkin Mash

We all know that salmon is a winner of a dish. This is both a great and easy way to do it — served on a light bed of lime-infused sweet mash. Great colours on the plate and great tasting! Thanks to my brother-in-law, Guy, for this terrific recipe!

Preparation time: 10 minutes   **Cooking time:** 20 minutes

Rating:

*Great colours
on the plate and
great tasting!*

Ingredients

2 salmon fillets, skin on

cracked pepper and salt

2 cm-square slice of butter plus 1/2 tbsp

1 lime, halved, 1 half cut into quarters with 2 wedges reserved for garnish; 1 half juiced

1 medium sweet potato, peeled and cut into 2 cm pieces

10 cm wedge of pumpkin, peeled and cut into 3 cm pieces

6 spears asparagus

1 small red capsicum, sliced into thin strips

Method

Season the salmon fillets on both sides with cracked pepper and salt.

Place sweet potato and pumpkin chunks into a saucepan and cover with water. Bring to the boil and cook until you can push a fork into the pieces easily, which will take about 10 minutes. Drain and return to saucepan. Mash with a fork, along with a 2 cm square piece of butter and the juice from a lime wedge. Cover to keep warm and set aside.

Trim the bottom 2 cm off each asparagus spear. Lay spears in a microwave-safe dish and top with sliced capsicum. Place dish in microwave on a rack with a container of water beneath it and cook at high power for 2 minutes. Alternatively, steam the asparagus and capsicum for 2 minutes. Cover and set aside.

Melt half a tablespoon of butter in a non-stick fry pan over medium heat. Just before the butter starts to brown, add the salmon fillets, skin side down. Cook until the bottom half of the fillet turns opaque, about 3 minutes. Squeeze 1 wedge of lime over the fillets and turn over. Cook for a further 2 to 3 minutes. Remove from heat.

To serve, place a helping of the mash on each warmed plate and top with 1 salmon fillet. Quickly add the juice of half a lime and a knob of butter to the fry pan over medium-high heat; stir until butter is melted. Spoon the lime butter over salmon and mash. Arrange the vegetables on the side of the plate and garnish with a small wedge of lime.

Wine suggestion: Yarra Valley Pinot Noir or, for white drinkers, try a Hunter Valley Verdelho

Lamb Back-Strap on Sweet Potato Mash
with Mustard and Red Wine Jus

You've got to love lamb. I think it's the law. Maybe I'm biased because I was brought up on a sheep farm, but there is something about lamb that makes it a real winner. Since the new cuts of lamb have come out, it has made it even easier to entertain — no more chasing a loin chop around the plate or trying to find the meat on a cutlet. This back-strap dish is great. I've received numerous compliments for this meal (thus its high pants drop rating). You can't beat the presentation, either.

Preparation time: 30 minutes   **Cooking time:** 20–30 minutes

Rating:

Since the new cuts of lamb have come out,
it has made it even easier to entertain —
no more chasing a loin chop around the plate.

Ingredients

lamb back-strap, about 5 cm by 15 to 20 cm, or sirloin

1 tbsp olive oil, plus more for stir-frying

2–3 sprigs of rosemary, leaves stripped and chopped finely

sea salt

cracked pepper

3/4 cup chicken stock

1/3 cup red wine (drinkable; never cook with rubbish!)

1 tsp seeded mustard

splash of Worcestershire sauce

1 sweet potato, peeled and cut into 4 cm pieces

3 potatoes, peeled and cut into 4 cm pieces

knob of butter

seasonal vegetables, chopped for stir-frying (suggestions include celery, green beans, carrots, onions and mushrooms)

1 tsp sesame oil

ground Chinese five-spice

1 tsp corn flour, mixed into paste with 1 tbsp cold water (alternatively, blend a dab of butter with plain flour to form a 1 cm ball; can be made ahead of time and kept in the fridge)

Method

Preheat oven to 180° C.

Rub the lamb with olive oil to coat. Mix the chopped rosemary with some salt and pepper. Press this mixture over the entire surface of the lamb. Cover with cling wrap and set aside for 15–30 minutes at room temperature.

Start the sauce by heating the chicken stock and red wine in a small saucepan over medium heat. Stir in the mustard and Worcestershire sauce and bring to a boil. Simmer to reduce by half, stirring occasionally. This will take about 15-20 minutes by which stage the potatoes and lamb will be cooked.

Cover potatoes with cold water in a saucepan and bring to a boil. Boil 15–20 minutes until tender (when you can push a fork into them). Drain. Mash with butter, pepper and salt to taste. Cover to keep warm and set aside.

While the potatoes are cooking, sear the lamb on a very hot, heavy-duty fry pan, griddle or barbecue over high heat. (The pan must be very hot before adding the lamb or it won't sear and lock in the juices.) Brown lamb evenly on all sides, about 1 minute per side. Place lamb on a baking tray and cook in the oven for 10 minutes. Don't overcook! The lamb should be pink in the centre. Remove from the oven and cover loosely with foil, to rest.

Preheat a wok with a combination of olive and sesame oil. Stir-fry harder vegetables first, such as onions, carrots, celery and other root vegetables for 2 minutes, and then add softer vegetables, such as mushrooms, for 1 minute. Don't overcook,

as you want the vegetables to have a bit of crunch left to them. Sprinkle with a generous pinch of Chinese five-spice. Remove from heat and cover to keep warm.

Drain any residual juices from lamb platter into saucepan with simmering wine/ stock mixture. If sauce has not thickened sufficiently, add a teaspoon of corn flour that has been mixed with a tablespoon of cold water into a paste or the butter/ flour ball and stir until slightly thickened. Remove from heat.

To serve, scoop mashed potato onto warmed plates. Slice the back-strap on an angle into 1–2 cm slices and overlap the slices on top of the mashed potatoes. Drizzle with sauce. Serve with vegetables alongside.

Wine suggestion: Cabernet Sauvignon (from Coonawarra, in particular), Cabernet/Shiraz or Zinfandel

T-bone on Butter Bean Mash with Balsamic Mushroom and Tarragon Sauce

Beef on the bone has a really distinctive taste and a T-bone is great as it offers several different textures of meat in one cut: fillet (tenderloin) and strip loin (sirloin). Here, we set the T-bone on a light and tasty butter bean mash and top it with a lovely balsamic mushroom and tarragon sauce. You and your lucky dinner guest will love it!

Preparation time: 5 minutes   **Cooking time:** 30 minutes

Rating:

Ingredients

3 tbsp olive oil, divided into 2 tbsp and 1 tbsp

20 small mushrooms (Swiss browns are best), washed, ends trimmed

1 cup beef stock

2 tbsp balsamic vinegar

3 tsp brown sugar

1 tbsp chopped fresh tarragon or 1 tsp dried

100 ml full cream

2 T-bone steaks, at room temperature (remove from refrigerator 30 minutes ahead)

cracked salt and pepper

400 g tin butter beans, rinsed well and drained

1 tbsp butter

You and your
lucky dinner guest
will love it!

Method

Place 2 tablespoons of olive oil in a fry pan over medium heat. Add the mushrooms and sauté gently for 5 minutes till nicely browned. Remove mushrooms from pan and set aside. Increase heat to medium-high. To the pan, add the beef stock, balsamic vinegar and brown sugar. Boil gently till the fluid has reduced by half (about 10 minutes). Add the mushrooms back to the pan along with the tarragon and cream. Stir well and simmer for 2 minutes. Remove from heat and set aside.

Season steaks with cracked salt and pepper on both sides. Heat up your barbecue or fry pan with 1 tablespoon of olive oil. Depending on thickness of steaks, cook about 3–4 minutes each side, without nudging or turning. For a medium steak, turn when you see a small amount of blood coming through the surface.

Meanwhile, cover butter beans with water in a medium saucepan. Bring to the boil and boil gently for 3 minutes. Drain; return to saucepan off the heat. Add the butter and mash until smooth. Cover and set aside.

When the steaks are fully cooked, set on a warm plate and cover tightly with aluminium foil. Let rest for 3 minutes.

Meanwhile warm your plates and turn the heat back on low under the sauce. Spoon some butter bean mash on each plate. Lay the steak half on, half off the mash, and spoon a liberal amount of the mushroom sauce over both the steak and the mash. Serve with a tossed salad or steamed vegetables.

Wine suggestion: A lovely Barossa Shiraz will prove the perfect match for this beautiful meal.

Chicken and Mushroom Risotto

Risotto is a very impressive dish to make. It may look really hard to master but, in fact, it's actually pretty easy! And you don't need to serve any side dishes as everything goes into the rice so what could be easier or more convenient, yet still come out looking like a restaurant-calibre meal?

The key thing is to keep the stock you're adding hot the whole time, so that the cooking temperature stays consistent and doesn't drop, like it would if you added the stock cold. You also need to keep stirring regularly (but not constantly, as some cooks would like you to believe). The colours and flavours in this complement each other really well and it's a hearty dish. Plus, once you master the basic technique for risotto, there are endless varieties you can try, from vegetable to meat to seafood, and even just fresh herbs. What are you waiting for? Go for it!

Preparation time: 10–15 minutes   **Cooking time:** 25 minutes

Rating:

The colours and flavours in this complement each other really well and it's a hearty dish.

Ingredients

4 cups chicken stock

1 tbsp soy sauce

1 tbsp olive oil, plus more for frying

3 chicken thighs, fat removed and chopped into 2 cm cubes

Dried mixed herbs, dried thyme, salt and cracked black pepper

1 medium onion, finely chopped

2 cloves of garlic, finely chopped

1 cm slice of butter

2 cups uncooked Arborio or Carnaroli rice (no substitutes!)

1 cup dry white wine

10 cm length of golden (kumera) sweet potato, chopped into ½–1 cm cubes

5 mushrooms, wiped clean with a damp paper towel and cut into quarters

12 snow peas, trimmed (tips cut off) and cut in thirds

1/4 cup freshly grated Parmesan cheese

50 ml full cream

Method

Combine chicken stock with soy sauce in medium saucepan. Bring to boil. Lower heat and let sit just below a simmer. (Do this literally on a back burner so it's out of your way.)

In a large, deep fry pan over medium-high heat, lightly brown chicken pieces in olive oil. Toss in a liberal amount of mixed herbs, thyme and salt/pepper. Remove from pan and set aside in small bowl. Add 1 tablespoon olive oil to pan over medium-low heat. Sauté onion and garlic together, until onion is slightly translucent, while being careful not to brown the garlic or it will become bitter.

Raise the heat to medium-high and add the butter. When melted, add the rice and stir to coat the rice in the melted butter. Cook for 90 seconds until you see a white dot appear in the centre of the rice grains. Add the cup of wine and stir until nearly absorbed. Lower heat to medium-low again.

Add 1 cup of hot chicken stock, stirring frequently. As soon as it is nearly absorbed, add stock a cupful at a time, stirring frequently. Do not add more until the previous amount is fully absorbed. (One good way to judge is to think how beach sand looks after the seawater has receded; it gets that same slightly dimpled look to its surface.)

After the second cup of stock is absorbed, add the sweet potato chunks. Continue to add the stock, stirring frequently to prevent sticking.

When you are ready to add the last cup of stock, add the mushrooms and chicken. Keep stirring. When the last of the stock is almost completely absorbed, add the snow peas, cream and Parmesan cheese. Remove from heat, stir and let sit for 1 minute. Heat the serving plates and serve immediately with additional grated Parmesan and cracked pepper.

Wine suggestion: Semillon/Sauvignon Blanc or unoaked Chardonnay

Spaghetti with Oven-Roasted Capsicum and Tomato Pesto, Shredded Chicken and Mushrooms

This little dish is deceptively easy, but yet so very good. Quick, yet looks great and tastes even greater. Your guest is sure to be impressed. Lucky you're carbo-loading!

Preparation time: 15 minutes   **Cooking time:** 15 minutes

Rating:

This little dish is deceptively easy, but yet so very good.

Ingredients

1 medium-large red capsicum, quartered

60 g semi-dried tomatoes

10–15 g shredded Parmesan cheese

1 large garlic clove

juice of 1 small lemon

2 tbsp olive oil

breast from 1/2 pre-cooked chicken

250 g thin spaghetti, such as cappellini

10 g butter

4 mushrooms, peeled and quartered

salt and pepper

40 g feta, crumbled

fresh parsley sprigs, chopped or whole, for garnish (optional)

Method

Preheat grill on high.

Place capsicum skin side up under the grill on a baking tray for 10 minutes or until capsicum quarters are charred and blistered. Using tongs, insert capsicum into a plastic bag and seal for 5 minutes (this helps lift the skin off the capsicum). Then remove from the bag, peel off the skin and discard. Place the peeled capsicum into a blender or food processor and puree with semi-dried tomatoes, Parmesan and garlic. Process ingredients until nicely chopped, and then add the lemon juice and the olive oil. Process till it reaches a nice paste consistency.

Place chicken breast meat onto cutting board and shred coarsely into strips. Set aside.

Boil water for pasta; add 1 teaspoon salt when it comes to a boil. Cook spaghetti until it is *al dente,* according to package directions.

Meanwhile, melt butter in a small fry pan over medium heat. Sauté mushrooms for 2 minutes, season with pepper and salt, remove from heat and set aside.

Drain pasta once cooked; return to saucepan. Add the tomato-pepper puree and mix to coat the pasta. Then add the shredded chicken and mushrooms and stir gently.

On a couple of warmed plates, serve up a portion of the pasta mix. Make sure there are both mushrooms and chicken in each serving. Sprinkle with crumbled feta and garnish with chopped parsley.

Wine suggestion: Hunter Valley Verdelho for the white lovers and a Sangiovese blend for those red fans.

Pepper-Crusted Salmon with Lime and Coriander Vinaigrette

Citrus and fish were meant to be together! The zing of the lime gives the fish a nice kick and the coriander, the king of herbs, provides a subtle, peppery heat.

The beauty of this dish, aside from the speed at which it can be rustled up, is the ratio of 1 lime per 2 tablespoons olive oil, which can be adjusted to suit how much lime zing you prefer.

This dish tastes sensational and looks beautiful, as if a heck of a lot more work went into it than actually did. Watch out pants — you're heading south!

Tip: For speed and convenience, use a blender to puree the vinaigrette. The oil and lime will emulsify to an appealing mint green colour and meld the flavours nicely. Alternatively, hand chopping gives a chunkier, homemade texture that you may prefer.

Preparation time: 15 minutes **Cooking time:** 15 minutes

Rating:

Ingredients

2 limes, preferably unwaxed, with flesh that yields slightly (tip: heavy limes contain more juice)

1 clove garlic, peeled and chopped

2 level tsp coarsely ground (wholegrain) mustard

6 tbsp olive oil, divided

salt and black pepper

handful of fresh coriander, woody stems removed, leaves chopped

6 new potatoes, halved

1 heaped tbsp whole mixed peppercorns, coarsely crushed*

1 heaped tbsp plain flour, seasoned with salt

2 seven-ounce pieces of fish, such as salmon, spangled emperor or coral trout

20 green beans, topped and tailed (ends pinched off)

*Placing peppercorns inside cling wrap or plastic food storage bag before crushing with a mallet or rolling pin keeps them from shooting across the room!

Method

To prepare vinaigrette, grate the limes, taking care not to grate the white pith beneath the rind. Reserve zest (rind). Juice the limes. (Pressing down with your hand while rolling them first on a firm surface to soften crushes the cells and releases the juice more easily.)

Crush the chopped garlic in a bowl. Stir in mustard, lime zest, lime juice, 4 tablespoons of olive oil, salt and pepper to taste, and chopped coriander. (Alternatively, put all ingredients in a blender or food processor and puree.) Set aside.

Fill a medium saucepan half-full with water and bring to a boil. When the water is boiling, add salt and the potatoes. Boil 10 minutes or until potatoes are tender (i.e., you can stick a fork into them). Drain. Put potatoes back in saucepan, covered, off the heat.

Combine the coarsely crushed peppercorns, salt and flour. Skin fish if desired (for salmon, leave skin intact) and coat with seasoned flour. Shake off any excess.

While the potatoes are cooking, heat 1 tablespoon olive oil in a large fry pan over medium-high heat. When hot (a drop of water added to the pan should instantly sizzle; if it dances or jumps, the pan is too hot), add the fish and fry 2 to 3 minutes on one side until crisp. Remove fish, add another tablespoon of olive oil, and then flip to fry other side. Salmon, depending on your preference, should be a nice pink colour on the inside but heated through. Try to use fillets of comparable size and thickness to ensure cooking time remains consistent and the fillets finish cooking at the same time.

When the fish is cooked on both sides, pour the vinaigrette into the hot pan around the fish. Remove pan from heat and let vinaigrette continue to simmer so the sauce reduces. Spoon some of it over the fish whilst still in the pan.

Meanwhile, place the beans in the microwave and cook at 100% power for 90 seconds, or bring a saucepan of water to a boil and add the beans, cooking for 3 minutes. (If you don't have a microwave, take a moment to add a microwave to your Christmas wish list!)

Serve fish on warmed plates with new potatoes and green beans. In summer, a baby leaf green salad makes a nice accompaniment instead of the potatoes. Use a spoonful of the vinaigrette to dress the salad.

Wine suggestion: Eden Valley Riesling

This dish tastes sensational and looks beautiful, as if a heck of a lot more work went into it than actually did.

Moroccan Lamb Shanks

Another great comfort food. (It's criminal now to think that we once threw these cuts of meat to the dogs!) Patient cooking in a slow cooker, casserole dish or tagine brings out the best in this meat. The end result is a rich, thick sauce with beautifully tender meat that practically falls off the bone by itself. This version has a lovely Moroccan twist, thanks to the eggplant, chickpeas and apricots.

Prep time: 20 minutes   **Cooking time:** 3 hours

Rating:

Another great comfort food.

Ingredients

olive oil

4 lamb shanks, preferably French trimmed

1 medium eggplant, cubed into 1 to 2 cm pieces

1 stalk of celery, chopped

1 carrot, chopped

1 medium onion, chopped

400 g tin of chopped tomatoes

1 medium tin chick peas, drained

1/2 cup chopped dried apricots

1 tbsp tomato paste

3 cloves garlic, finely chopped

5 cm piece of ginger, peeled and finely chopped

1 cinnamon stick

2 cloves

1 small chilli, finely chopped

2 tsp each of ground cumin and ground coriander

1/2 tsp smoked paprika

500 ml beef stock

125 ml dry white wine

1 cup water

1 tsp salt

1 cup couscous grains

salt and pepper to taste

Method

Preheat oven to 200° C.

At the same time, preheat barbecue or heat some olive oil in a heavy-based fry pan over medium-high heat (I prefer the barbecue). Brown the shanks all over and then transfer them to an ovenproof casserole dish (or tagine, if you have one).

Add the chopped vegetables to the dish, along with the tinned vegetables, apricots and tomato paste. Then add the garlic, ginger, cinnamon, cloves, chilli, cumin, coriander and paprika. Pour the stock and white wine over meat and vegetables and stir well.

Place shanks in oven and cook for 1 hour. Check to see that the shanks are well submerged under the liquid. Cook for an additional hour; salt and pepper to taste. Reduce oven temperature to 180° C and return the dish to the oven for a further hour (uncovered if the liquid needs thickening). By the end of the third hour, the meat should be falling off the bone.

With 10 minutes to go, boil 1 cup of water in a medium saucepan with 2 tablespoons of olive oil. Add salt. Bring it to the boil and then turn off the heat. Add couscous grains and stir. Cover and let sit for 3 minutes. Add a small amount of butter and separate the grains using a fork. It should end up nice and fluffy.

Place a decent serve of couscous onto warmed plates and top with the lamb shanks and a generous serving of the vegetables and sauce.

Wine suggestion: Coonawarra Cabernet Sauvignon

Thai Pumpkin Soup

As we head into the cooler months, there is nothing better than soup to fill the space in hungry stomachs. This soup is great either as a starter or as a main dish.

Pumpkin soup is one of my all time favourites, and this little variation, with the added Thai spices, will melt the resistance of any maiden suffering the effects of frost!

Preparation time: 15 minutes   **Cooking time:** 45 minutes

Rating:

Ingredients

2 tbsp olive or vegetable oil

1 onion, cut into medium-sized pieces

1/2 butternut pumpkin, peeled and cut into medium-sized pieces

2 medium potatoes, peeled and cut into quarters

2 level tbsp red Thai curry paste

1 stalk of celery, cut into small pieces

1 tomato, de-seeded and chopped into small pieces

ground salt and pepper

1 litre vegetable stock

250 ml tin coconut milk

fresh coriander sprigs, chopped, for garnish (optional)

This soup is great either as a starter or as a main dish.

Method

Heat the oil in a large, deep saucepan over medium heat and add the onion, pumpkin and potato pieces. Add the red curry paste and stir well for 1 minute. Add the celery and tomato; stir well. Add a sprinkle of salt and cracked pepper. Add the vegetable stock and increase heat to medium-high. Simmer for at least 20 minutes or more, until the vegetables are very soft, stirring frequently to ensure nothing sticks to the bottom of the saucepan.

Using a blender or a hand held stick blender, carefully blend the hot contents of the saucepan to a smooth consistency. If using a blender, return soup to saucepan and heat over medium-low heat. Add the coconut milk and blend well. Increase heat slightly and simmer for a further 15 minutes, stirring regularly.

Serve in deep bowls along with some crusty bread rolls or slices from a breadstick.

Wine suggestion: Yarra Valley Pinot Noir

Green Thai Chicken Curry

There's something about cooking Asian food — it's not our normal Aussie fare and it has a slightly mysterious feel. It's tasty and spicy without being unbearably hot. South East Asia also evokes visions of secluded, unspoiled beaches, great food, exciting holidays and new experiences, so it's a great conversation starter for a great meal. This version has a slightly thicker sauce than those in traditional Thai restaurants. If you prefer a thinner sauce, do not flour the chicken pieces. Either way, it's a sure-fire way to heat things up between you!

Preparation time: 10 minutes   **Cooking time:** 45 minutes

Rating:

South East Asia also evokes visions of secluded, unspoiled beaches, great food, exciting holidays and new experiences, so it's a great conversation starter for a great meal.

Ingredients

olive oil

sesame oil

1 red onion, chopped into 1 to 2 cm pieces

300 g chicken, preferably dark meat (it's time to skip the breasts in favour of thighs here, boys!), chopped into 2 cm cubes

1/2 cup flour

400 ml tin of coconut milk

2–3 tbsp green curry paste

2 tbsp brown sugar

3 tsp fish sauce

1 small carrot, halved lengthwise, chopped into 3 mm pieces

1 medium green capsicum pepper, chopped into 2 to 3 cm pieces

2 tsp kaffir lime leaves, chopped finely (optional; these can be found pre-packaged in glass jars)

4 medium mushrooms, washed and quartered

1-1/2 cups jasmine rice (can be cooked ahead and reheated in microwave just before serving)

50–100 ml water for thinning sauce, if needed

fresh coriander (optional)

Method

Place olive and sesame oils into a large saucepan over medium-low heat. Cook onions until opaque in colour; they will break up as they cook.

Meanwhile dust chicken with flour (using a plastic bag makes this a less messy process!) Shake off excess flour and place on a plate. (Skip this step if you prefer a thinner sauce.)

Add the coconut milk, green curry paste, brown sugar and fish sauce to the onions. Mix well. Increase heat and bring to a boil. Turn down the heat and add the chicken. Cover and lightly simmer for 10 minutes.

Add the chopped carrots and cook another 5 minutes covered. Then add the capsicum and cook for another 5 minutes. Then add the kaffir lime leaves and mushrooms. Simmer for another 10-15 minutes.

Prepare the rice by pouring boiling water over rice in a saucepan set over low heat. The water should cover it by half a centimetre. Cover saucepan and cook for 12 minutes. Do not remove the lid during the cooking process. Check after 12 minutes, fluffing it with a fork. If all the water has been absorbed and the rice is cooked (taste it!), then turn heat off and set aside, covered for 2 minutes, to settle. If not cooked add a few tablespoons of boiling water and continue to cook over low heat until tender.

Once rice is done, warm your bowls by rinsing them with boiling water. Empty and wipe dry. Fill with rice, topped with the chicken curry, with a good dose of the sauce. Chop some fresh coriander and sprinkle on top.

Wine suggestion: Yarra Valley Pinot Gris

Beef and Noodle Stir-Fry

This one is definitely from the 'keep it simple' school of cooking. One advantage is that you can even throw this together after a few beers at the pub because it's quick and easy. And cooking is a heck of a lot healthier than settling for some rubbish takeout or fast food. Your date will be impressed when you demonstrate you can whip together such a tasty meal in no time at all after an evening out, which definitely makes it a high scorer on the pants off scale. Tip: Don't skimp on quality; use a good cut of meat here.

Preparation time: 20 minutes **Cooking time**: 10 minutes

Rating:

One advantage is that you
can even throw this together after
a few beers at the pub because
it's quick and easy.

Ingredients

300 g beef or veal strips (I typically finely cut 2 rib eye minute steaks for my strips)

50 ml soy sauce

50 ml sweet chilli sauce, or sweet chilli and ginger sauce

1 small onion, halved, then finely sliced

1 small red capsicum, sliced into fine strips

1 celery stalk, cut into thin 5 cm strips

4–5 mushrooms, skinned, quartered

2-1/2 tbsp olive oil, divided

1–2 tsp sesame oil

20 ml sweet soy sauce, such as Indonesian-style kecap manis

pinch of Chinese five-spice (optional)

1/3 cup chicken stock

450 g package of thick hokkien noodles

Method

Marinate beef strips in soy sauce and sweet chilli sauce, turning to coat thoroughly. Refrigerate covered for 20 minutes (can be less if you're really in a hurry).

Meanwhile, place noodles in a large bowl and cover with boiling water. Let sit for 2 minutes. Using a fork, separate noodles carefully and thoroughly; then drain.

In a large fry pan or wok, heat 1 tablespoon of olive oil with 1 teaspoon of sesame oil over medium-high heat. Add half the meat, removing it from marinade using a slotted spoon to drain off excess and quickly brown for 1 minute. Remove and set aside in separate bowl. Repeat with the remaining meat, adding more oil if necessary.

Add the onions to the wok, followed by the capsicum, celery and, lastly, mushrooms and stir-fry for 2 to 3 minutes. Add a pinch of Chinese five-spice and a splash of both soy and olive oil to the wok to keep surface moist.

Add both the noodles and meat to the vegetables and mix together well. Add remaining marinade, stock and kecap manis and simmer for 1 to 2 minutes. The marinade must boil, as it was in contact with the raw meat. Serve.

Wine suggestion: Shiraz/Viognier blend

Pork Cutlets in Plum, Red Wine and Mustard Sauce

We all probably remember those pork ads that appeared years ago on television: "Get some pork on your fork!" It was suggestive, seductive and the girl in the ad looked like she was waiting for one of us bachelors to cook it for her. With this great recipe, your cooking will live up to those expectations. So go ahead. The person of your dreams is just waiting for you to start cooking!

Preparation time: 5 minutes   **Cooking time:** 40 minutes

Rating:

The person of your dreams
is just waiting for you
to start cooking!

Ingredients

4 pork cutlets, trimmed

2 tbsp plain flour

salt and pepper

1/2 cup prepared Asian plum sauce (a jar of SPC works well)

1/4 cup soy sauce

1 tbsp wholegrain mustard

1/2 cup red wine or port

1/4 cup olive oil, plus more for frying

1 tsp sesame oil (optional)

Asian greens, such as bok choy or pak choy, stalks and leaves separated and chopped

1 head of fresh broccolini

1 cup Jasmine rice grains

Method

Preheat oven to 180° C.

Dredge the pork cutlets in seasoned flour. (The easiest method is to put flour, salt and pepper into a plastic sandwich bag and shake each cutlet separately inside.) Dust off excess flour.

Heat up half a tablespoon of olive oil in a fry pan over medium heat and brown the pork for 1 minute on each side. Set browned pieces in an ovenproof dish. Deglaze the pan over the heat by adding the red wine, scraping up all the browned bits and mixing into the wine.

Whisk together the plum sauce, soy sauce, olive oil and mustard, and add to wine. Simmer for 10 minutes or until slightly thickened.

Pour the sauce from the fry pan over the pork cutlets. Cover with aluminium foil to prevent pork from drying out in the oven and roast for 10 minutes. Remove the foil, flip the cutlets and roast for another 5 minutes. Remove from the oven and cover with foil to keep warm.

Meanwhile, cover jasmine rice in a saucepan with boiling water to a level of about 3 mm above rice. Cover and cook over very low heat for 10–12 minutes.

Preheat a wok with 1 tablespoon of olive oil mixed with 1 teaspoon of sesame oil. Add chopped stalk pieces from the Asian greens and stir-fry for 60 seconds, then add the broccolini for 30 seconds and then add the leafy ends for another 60 seconds. Remove from heat and cover to keep warm.

To serve, spoon a bed of rice on each warmed plate. Top with 1 or 2 of the pork cutlets and spoon plum sauce on top of cutlets. Arrange vegetables on each side of cutlets alongside rice and serve to your grinning dinner guest. The smell is gorgeous and the appearance very impressive.

Wine suggestion: Cabernet Sauvignon/ Merlot blend.

Osso Bucco (Veal Shanks)

Osso bucco is the beef equivalent of lamb shanks. It smells great while you're cooking and tastes really wonderful on a cold evening when comfort food is just the ticket. I didn't really appreciate just how warm and comfortable this meal could make a girl feel until I tried it out.

Match this dish with an earthy red wine and you've got a winner on your hands. It does take a little more preparation and cooking time than some of the other recipes in this book, but let me assure you, the time and effort spent is well worth it! This meal tastes even better the next day, so the recipe has been adjusted to provide you with leftovers to enjoy while you are reliving those special moments from the night before.

Preparation time: 20 minutes   **Cooking time:** 2 hours

Rating:

Ingredients

4-6 large veal shanks, patted dry with paper towel

salt and pepper

1/2 cup of flour, in a plastic bag for shaking

7 or more tbsp unsalted butter, divided into 3 tbsp, 3 tbsp and 1 tbsp

5 tbsp olive oil, divided into 3 tbsp and 2 tbsp

1-1/2 cups dry white wine

1-1/2 medium onions, finely chopped

1 large carrot, finely chopped

2 celery stalks, finely chopped

3 cloves garlic, finely chopped

2-1/2 cups of beef stock

2 tbsp tomato paste

3 large ripe tomatoes, chopped, or 1 400 g tin of chopped tomatoes

5 sprigs each of parsley and thyme chopped, (or substitute 1/2 tbsp dried mixed herbs)

1 bay leaf

2 tsp lemon or orange zest (grated skin of the orange/lemon, coloured part only)

1 cup couscous grains

1 cup boiling water

*Match this dish with
an earthy red wine and you've
got a winner on your hands.*

Method

Preheat oven to 200° C.

Season the veal shanks with salt and pepper. Coat in the flour and shake off excess.

In a heavy fry pan, melt 3 tablespoons of butter in 3 tablespoons of olive oil over a medium-high heat. Brown the shanks in batches, adding additional butter and oil if necessary. Transfer browned shanks to an ovenproof casserole dish. Pour 1 cup of white wine into the fry pan and boil, scraping up the browned bits on the bottom of the pan. (This is called 'deglazing the pan'.) Boil until liquid is reduced to about half a cup. Pour into the casserole dish. Cool fry pan slightly.

Melt 3 tablespoons of butter in fry pan over medium-low heat and cook the onion, carrots, celery and garlic, stirring occasionally, until softened. Do not allow vegetables to brown. Add the remaining 1/2 cup of white wine, beef stock, tomato paste, tomatoes, parsley, thyme, bay leaf and citrus zest. Add a small amount of salt and pepper to taste (not too much — more can be added at the end if needed). Increase heat to medium-high and simmer for 10 minutes.

Pour vegetable mixture into the casserole dish, mixing gently with the shanks. Cover and place dish in oven. Cook for 90 minutes, stirring and turning the shanks every 30 minutes.

During the last 20 minutes of cooking, bring 1 cup of water to a boil in a medium saucepan over high heat. When boiling, add 2 tablespoons of olive oil and a pinch of salt. Remove from heat, add couscous grains and stir. Cover and let sit for 3 minutes. Remove the lid and add a tablespoon of butter; gently stir with a fork to separate any clumps.

Serve couscous on warmed dinner plates and top with shanks. Ladle a generous helping of vegetables and sauce over the shanks and couscous. Sprinkle with zest and chopped parsley. Serve with a proud smile!

Wine suggestion: McLaren Vale Shiraz Grenache

Pasta Carbonara

We all love the classics and Carbonara is unquestionably one of them. This recipe is quick and not oily or heavy. Definitely the choice for women who only allow themselves to be wicked behind closed doors. For us blokes who don't mind when people see us indulging wantonly, well, who among us doesn't love the warm feeling this garlic, bacon and cream sauce gives us? Pass the Parmesan!

Preparation time: 5 minutes   **Cooking time:** 15 minutes

Rating:

Definitely the choice for women who only allow themselves to be wicked behind closed doors.

Ingredients

knob of butter, roughly a half-centimetre slice

1 tbsp olive oil

1 brown onion, finely chopped

2 cloves garlic, finely chopped

cracked pepper

2 rashers of middle bacon, rind removed, finely chopped

200 g dried fettuccine or farfalle pasta

200 ml thickened cream

1/4 cup freshly grated Parmesan cheese, plus more for serving

2 egg yolks* (use free range eggs for superior colour)

1 tbsp fresh parsley, chopped

*Separate yolks from whites by cracking the egg carefully in half over a small bowl, taking care to keep the yolk unbroken in one of the shells. Gently roll the yolk back and forth between the two shells, allowing the white to drip into the bowl until no more eggwhite remains. Drop yolk into a separate bowl. Discard eggwhite or freeze for another use.

Method

Melt butter and olive oil in a small fry pan over medium-low heat. Add onion and garlic and lightly fry with a pinch of cracked pepper till the onion separates and turns slightly translucent, roughly 3 to 4 minutes.

Increase heat to medium. Add bacon and fry until golden brown, about 5 minutes.

Whilst the bacon is frying, fill a medium saucepan 2/3 full with water and bring to a boil over high heat. Add 2 pinches of salt when it reaches a boil. (Salted water has a higher boiling point, so it takes longer to bring to a boil than unsalted water; always wait until the water boils before salting.) Boil pasta according to package directions, about 8–10 minutes.

To the bacon, add 175 ml of the cream, stir and bring to a simmer. Add 1/4 cup of freshly grated Parmesan, stirring. When sauce begins to thicken, remove from heat and cover if pasta is nearly finished cooking; otherwise, leave covered over a very low heat.

In a separate cup or bowl, lightly beat the egg yolks with a fork and add the remaining 25 ml cream to the eggs.

Drain the pasta and return it to the saucepan away from the heat. Immediately pour the egg mixture over the pasta. Stir it through to coat the pasta thoroughly and let it sit for 60 seconds, to allow the residual heat from the pasta to gently cook the egg. (If you do this on a heated surface, you'll end up with scrambled eggs, so don't do it!)

Now, add the sauce to the pasta. Stir gently but thoroughly, cover, and let sit for 30 seconds.

Serve into warm bowls and sprinkle with more grated Parmesan. Salt and pepper to taste. Garnish with parsley for an attractive presentation.

Wine suggestion: King Valley Sangiovese

Pants Off Salmon

The original deal sealer! It's got a book named after it — what more do we need to say?

Preparation time: 15 minutes **Cooking time:** 20 minutes

Rating:

The original deal sealer!

Ingredients

1/2 small red onion, very finely chopped

1/2 medium red chilli, very finely chopped

2 cm-square piece of ginger, peeled, very finely chopped

2–4 salmon fillets, skin on, comparably sized for even cooking

12 drops fish sauce

1 tbsp soy sauce

400 ml tin coconut cream or coconut milk

olive oil

1/2 to 2/3 cup rissoni pasta (resembles a large rice grain)

1 medium red capsicum, thinly sliced

2 large handfuls (150 g bag) baby leaf spinach

sesame oil (optional)

black pepper

Method

Preheat oven to 200° C. (180° C if using a fan-forced/convection oven.)

Lightly oil a fry pan or wok (an oil-soaked paper towel works well here) set over low heat.

Sauté chopped onion with chilli and ginger until soft and slightly opaque (cloudy). Remove from heat and transfer to an ovenproof baking dish with lid, just large enough to accommodate fillets without overcrowding. Cover bottom of dish evenly with mixture but be careful not to layer it

too thickly; you want a thin coating when you add the fillets.

Place the salmon fillets skin side up onto the onion/chilli/ginger mix.

Mix fish and soy sauces into coconut cream, blending well. Pour just enough coconut cream mix on top of salmon so that it just covers the top of the salmon. (You may not need the whole tin.)

Place lid on the baking dish and bake in oven for 15 minutes.

Meanwhile, fill a small saucepan halfway with water and bring to the boil. Place a small amount of salt into the boiling water. When only 10 minutes remain for the salmon to cook, add the pasta to the boiling water, adjusting heat to maintain a gentle boil, for about 6 minutes, until *al dente*. (*Al dente* is what the Italians call 'toothy' — slightly firm but not too chewy.) Drain; return to saucepan and cover, leave off the heat.

Oil the fry pan again, this time adding a bit of sesame oil, if available, and place over medium heat. Sauté red capsicum with a dash of soy sauce and ground black pepper for 1 minute. Add fresh spinach, reserving a small handful aside. When spinach is slightly wilted, remove from heat and cover with lid to keep warm.

When salmon has finished cooking (you want it still soft, with a little pink in the centre) remove from oven and peel skin off fillets.

Spread a layer of uncooked spinach leaves on each plate. Spoon a layer of rissoni onto the spinach leaves. Layer the cooked vegetables over the rissoni.

Gently slide the salmon onto the rissoni with the underside facing up to display the colourful onion/chilli/garlic mix embedded in the flesh. Ladle enough coconut sauce to dress fish without spilling too much over the plate.

The vivid colours of this dazzling dish will amaze your guest, and the exquisite taste will invariably have your guest wondering how to return the favour!

Wine suggestion: Adelaide Hill Sauvignon Blanc

Boil 2 medium potatoes until tender. Drain and return to saucepan.

While potatoes are boiling, heat some olive oil in a fry pan over medium heat. Brown the lamb rumps for 3–4 minutes on each side. They should be a golden brown colour, with a little pink remaining at the edges. Place in the oven on a separate tray alongside the beetroot to roast for 10 minutes. Remove lamb from oven, cover tightly with aluminium foil and set aside to rest for 5 minutes.

When the beetroot is soft, remove from the oven and take skin off. (You'll need an oven mitt to help as the beetroot is hot and, remember, beetroot stains!) Add beetroot to the potato along with the grated apple, 50 grams of butter and the milk and mash well. Add salt and pepper to taste. Cover to keep warm in the saucepan.

Steam ears of corn, or microwave covered with 1 tablespoon of water and cooked for 2 to 3 minutes on 100% power.

Strain solids from Cabernet sauce and discard.

To serve, spoon some of the mash over 2/3 of the plate, flattening the top slightly with the back of the spoon. Take a lamb rump and place onto the mash. Drizzle with the strained wine jus and set an ear of corn on the side, topped with a knob of butter.

Wine suggestion: Serve with the same Cabernet Sauvignon you made the jus with.

Steak and Garlic Prawns

This dish combines the best of both worlds — a great piece of meat topped with the beautiful sweetness of prawns. Paired with a lovely glass of red wine, such as a Shiraz, this will be sure to knock the socks off (not to mention any other stray garments) any guest at your digs — so choose your guest carefully! The potent garlic pretty much guarantees no one else will want to get too close to you that evening so make the most of it!

And guys, resist the temptation to over-handle the steaks or they may dry out and toughen up. You only need to turn the steaks once, not 50 times!

Preparation time: 30 minutes   **Cooking time:** 15 minutes

Rating:

This dish combines the best of both worlds — a great piece of meat topped with the beautiful sweetness of prawns.

Ingredients

3 cloves garlic, crushed or minced

7 tbsp olive oil, divided

8 to 12 medium to large raw green prawns, rinsed, peeled and de-veined, tails left intact

lettuce leaves, torn into shreds

cucumber, sliced

feta cheese, cubed or crumbled

cherry tomatoes, halved

2 tsp balsamic vinegar

1 tsp wholegrain or Dijon mustard

2 rib fillets, 2-1/2 cm thick (get your butcher to cut them; if they're too thin, they'll dry out)

salt and pepper

150 ml full or cooking cream

Method

Crush garlic and mix together with 3 tablespoons of the olive oil. Coat prawns with garlic/oil mixture and set aside in a bowl.

Combine lettuce, cucumber slices, crumbled feta and tomatoes in bowl. Mix balsamic vinegar, mustard and 4 tablespoon olive oil, blending well. Set aside. (If you plan to dress the salad in advance, do not do so until ready to serve or the lettuce may wilt prematurely.)

Pre-heat plate section on barbecue to high and then reduce to a medium heat when ready.

Season steaks with salt and pepper. Place steak onto barbecue. Men, again I caution you: do not play with your meat! The steak should only be turned once! For a medium-rare steak, when the blood rises through the uncooked surface, it is time to turn the steak over. Cook until this occurs again, about 3 to 5 minutes per side, depending on the thickness of the steak. Adjust cooking times slightly if a rarer or more well done steak is preferred. Immediately remove the steak from the barbecue to a pre-heated plate and cover to sit for 3 to 5 minutes, to permit the juices to return to the meat and keep it tender and juicy.

Once the steaks are underway, heat an oiled fry pan over high heat and cook garlic-coated prawns for 45-60 seconds. Turn prawns over and cook for an additional 45–60 seconds. Immediately add the cream and stir. Turn the heat off and let the prawns sit in the warm cream.

Place each steak on a pre-heated plate. Top with half of the prawns and drizzle any remaining creamy garlic sauce over the top. Serve with salad, either dressed or with dressing on the side. (FYI — we're talking about dressing the salad here. Any other state of dress or undress is entirely at your discretion.)

Wine suggestion: Barossa Shiraz

Chorizo and Butter Bean Stew

This is great for a casual evening supper, a tasty starter or a weekend lunch. And, like all stews, it is a cinch to prepare. Surprisingly filling, the stew will warm the stomach while your witty conversation will warm your guest's heart. If you prefer something a bit feistier, get your butcher to supply a chorizo picante, which has added chilli.

Preparation time: 10 minutes   **Cooking time:** 40–60 minutes

Rating:

Surprisingly filling, the stew will warm the stomach while your witty conversation will warm your guest's heart.

Ingredients

2 tbsp olive oil

1 brown onion, roughly chopped

2 cloves garlic, thinly sliced

1 stalk celery, chopped

1 leek, sliced (white and pale green parts only)

250 g chorizo, cut in half lengthways and sliced

1 tsp smoked paprika

175 ml red wine (drinkable!)

2 medium potatoes, peeled and diced

400 g tin butter beans, drained and rinsed

400 g tin chopped tomatoes

125 ml chicken stock

1 tbsp chopped thyme

salt

1 tbsp chopped flat leaf parsley

Method

Heat the olive oil in a large saucepan with a lid over medium heat and fry the onions and garlic for 1 minute, taking care not to let them brown. Add the celery and leek and fry until soft.

Add the chorizo and paprika and cook for 2 minutes. Add the red wine and cook until it has reduced by half.

Add the potato, butter beans, tomatoes, stock and thyme to the saucepan. Increase heat slightly and bring to the boil; simmer covered for at least 30 minutes, stirring occasionally. (If you can simmer longer, the flavours will meld even better.) Salt to taste.

To serve, ladle stew into a shallow bowl and sprinkle with the chopped flat leaf parsley. Serve with slices of French bread (baguette) cut into diagonal slices.

Wine suggestion: A nice, earthy Grenache or Shiraz/Grenache blend or a nice Tempranillo to continue the Spanish theme!

Roast Chicken — an oldie but a goodie!

Roasts are an old favourite and great with roast veggies and gravy. Roasts of another kind are highly rated (and amusing) but you must share them with a very good mate. I've given you an example of a chicken roast here; however lamb and beef are just as good. Just get your butcher to give you a nice piece of meat and enjoy. Probably best not to be served on a Sunday night as, being a work night, you mightn't have as much luck convincing your guest to stay over, no matter how good the dinner is. Although it is sure to keep you in the good books till the next meeting!

Preparation time: 5 minutes   **Cooking time:** 1 hour 25 minutes

(Additional prep work whilst chook is cooking.)

Rating:

Roasts are an old favourite and great with roast veggies and gravy.

Ingredients

1 whole chicken, size 13 or 14 (1.3 or 1.4 kg)

2 lemons, quartered

2 sprigs fresh rosemary

olive oil

salt and pepper (can substitute McCormick's Season-all Seasoning Salt™)

3 large potatoes, peeled and cut into serving sized pieces

1 sweet potato, peeled and cut into serving sized pieces

2 carrots, sliced into 5 cm sticks, no more than 2 cm thick

1 pumpkin, peeled and cut into serving sized pieces (only as much as you need)

handful of fresh green beans, topped and tailed (ends trimmed) and cut into 4 to 5 cm lengths

butter

flour

boiling water

1 teaspoon either apricot jam or tomato sauce

1/4 cup white wine (optional)

Method

Preheat oven to 200° C. Rinse the chicken cavity well with water. Remove neck and pat dry with paper towel.

Cut lemons (leave 1 quarter to use with beans). Place six of the lemon quarters in the cavity, along with the rosemary. Rub 1/4 over the chicken and then place into the cavity with the others. Tuck skin into cavity to cover up.

Lightly oil the bottom of a roasting tray. Place chicken in the pan breast side down and sprinkle with salt/pepper. Now, your total cooking time should be 25 minutes per 500 grams. Follow the cooking times shown below and adjust the final 50 minutes to accommodate your size of chicken.

Roast in oven for 25 minutes.

Whilst chicken is cooking, combine potato, sweet potato, carrot and pumpkin pieces in a large bowl, drizzle with olive oil and toss well to coat.

After chicken has roasted for 25 minutes, remove from the oven and lower temperature to 180° C. Turn chicken over so it is now sitting breast side up. Season with salt and pepper. Scatter vegetables around the chicken and return the roasting tray to oven for 50 minutes. (Remember to adjust cooking time to the weight of your bird — 25 minutes per 500 grams pre-cooked weight.)

Cut trimmed beans into pieces. Place in a microwave-safe dish with lid and squeeze remaining lemon quarter over it. Set a knob of butter on top of the beans, cover the dish and set aside. (This gets cooked after the chicken comes out of the oven, minutes before serving.)

Test chicken by inserting a skewer into the breast and pulling it back out. If the juice is clear, the chicken is fully cooked; if the juice is cloudy or slightly bloody place it back in the oven for 15-minute intervals until any juice runs clear. Place chicken on warm platter and cover tightly with foil.

If vegetables are done, transfer to warmed platter and cover to keep warm. If you prefer them crisper or more well done, increase oven temperature to 240° C and check them every 5 or 10 minutes.

What really makes a roast such a great dish is, in my opinion, the gravy. Lightly sprinkle the empty roasting tray with flour (or gravy flour). Add a little boiling water and stir over a low heat on the stove top, to make a paste, scraping up the browned bits as the pan heats. Add a little more boiling water until the pan is deglazed (that means that all the browned bits have been scraped off the pan into the liquid). Add the apricot jam or tomato sauce. You can also opt to add the white wine. Bring to a gentle boil and stir until desired consistency is reached. Remove from heat. Pour into a gravy boat/dish to keep warm.

Place the beans in their covered dish in the microwave, leaving a slight gap to vent any steam, and cook on medium-high power for 2 to 3 minutes.

Carve the chicken and plate up with vegetables alongside. Add the beans and serve with the gravy.

Wine suggestion: Chardonnay, such as Cape Mentelle from Western Australia.

Greek Lamb

This recipe was very kindly supplied to me by my long-time bachelor mate, Gary. This lamb dish proved too much for one lovely young lady and they are now engaged. Proof that cooking dinner can certainly lead to romance!

Preparation time: 5 minutes   **Cooking time:** 130 minutes

Rating:

*Proof that cooking dinner can
certainly lead to romance!*

Ingredients

1-1/3 kg leg of lamb

1-1/2 lemons (1 chopped up for the potatoes, 1/2 juiced for lamb and yoghurt dressing)

salt and pepper

1/4 cup dry white wine

8 to 12 new potatoes (chopped in halves or quarters, depending on size) or 3 medium potatoes chopped into 2 cm by 2 cm chunks

olive oil

chopped fresh oregano and rosemary

1-1/3 cup water (1 cup for lamb; 1/3 cup for beans)

1 medium brown onion, chopped finely

2 medium carrots, sliced crosswise finely

2 cloves garlic, chopped finely

200 g green beans, trimmed (if using tinned, drain well)

400 g tin chopped or diced tomato

250 g Greek yoghurt

3 heads of fresh parsley, finely chopped

1 green cucumber, deseeded and sliced finely

Method

Preheat oven to 220° C.

Place lamb in a roasting tray, drizzle with olive oil and season with salt and black pepper. Add a generous squeeze of lemon juice and pour the dry white wine over the meat. Cook for 30 minutes.

Remove from oven and lower oven temperature to 175° C. Add the chunks of potato, sprinkled with salt and pepper, and the chopped lemon to the tray around the meat. Sprinkle a generous amount of freshly chopped oregano and rosemary over meat and potatoes.

Add 1 cup of water, cover roasting tray with foil and cook for an additional 90 minutes.

Meanwhile, in a medium saucepan, sauté 1 diced onion with the garlic over medium heat for several minutes. Lower heat if garlic starts to brown. Add sliced carrots, followed by green beans and chopped tomatoes. Season with salt and pepper and add 1/3 cup of water. Mix together well.

Immediately pour mixture into an oven-safe dish, cover with foil and cook for 1 hour at 175° C degrees (add to oven with lamb during last hour of cooking).

Once done, remove the leg of lamb and the beans from the oven. Increase oven temperature to 200° C. Place lamb on a carving tray/plate for 10 minutes, tented loosely with foil to rest. Return potatoes to oven for 10 more minutes, until done; remove. Place remaining liquid in a gravy dish to serve over meat and veggies.

In a small bowl, mix Greek yoghurt, finely chopped parsley, cucumber, a squeeze of lemon juice, salt and pepper.

Carve up the lamb. Place sliced lamb, potatoes and veggies onto dinner plates. Top with Greek yoghurt dressing or serve separately.

Wine suggestion: Coonawarra Cabernet Sauvignon is always a great complement to lamb.

Poached Chicken with Mango and Brie

My mate, Pete Knight, supplied me with this recipe, which he likes for many reasons. It tastes good, it's very simple to prepare and, if you're trying to impress a girl, it works very well. (Just ask Pete!) This is because, typically, if you offer to cook, people expect you to grill, fry or bake. I can guarantee you that 99% of people have not only never cooked chicken this way but also have never seen anyone else do it either. And, if you treat chicken in such a thoughtful, special way, well, then, you can be sure they'll be imagining the special way you might treat them as well!

Preparation time: 20 minutes   **Cooking time:** 20-25 minutes

Rating:

...if you treat chicken in such a thoughtful, special way, well, then, you can be sure they'll be imagining the special way you might treat them as well!

Ingredients

2 chicken breasts, as plump as you can find, butterflied (see instructions below)

2–4 thin slices of fresh mango

2–4 thin strips from a wedge of brie (cheese)

4 rashers of bacon or prosciutto (preferred)

salt and pepper

3 medium potatoes, peeled and cut into 3 cm pieces

milk

butter

2 ears of corn, halved crosswise

12 snow pea pods

Method

Take each chicken breast and slice through the middle lengthwise, leaving about 1 cm of flesh on one side. Open them up like a book and lay flat.

Take 1 slice of mango and 1 strip of brie and place atop 1 side of each chicken breast. Salt and pepper to taste.

Close the chicken, tucking the brie and mango inside. Add more or take out as required. Wrap 2 rashers of bacon or prosciutto around each breast.

Double-fold a piece of foil to a size of about 30 cm x 30 cm (do this twice), and place 1 breast of chicken in centre of each piece of foil. You will be boiling the chicken in the foil so the idea is to ensure it is tightly and securely wrapped to prevent the water from seeping inside and reaching the chicken. Do this by pinching the foil together around the edges with the breast so it forms a rectangular pocket. Then roll it up tightly so that it fits snugly around the chicken. Twist the ends like a bon-bon. (Don't be tempted to just fold the ends, as it will not be watertight.) Once sealed, roll it on the work surface until it is cylindrical in shape, careful not to tear the foil.

Fill a medium saucepan large enough to hold both chicken breasts halfway with water and bring to the boil over a medium-high heat. Place the foil packets containing the chicken and boil for 20 minutes, keeping chicken submerged as well as possible. (Try resting a small saucer in the water on top of the chicken packets).

Meanwhile, cover potatoes with water in a separate saucepan and bring to a boil over medium-high heat. Add salt to water and boil potatoes 15–20 minutes until tender when pierced with a fork. Drain. Add a knob of butter, some cracked pepper and mash well with a fork. Add a small amount of milk, 1 tablespoon at a time and continue to mash until desired consistency is reached.

Place corn halves in microwave-safe dish and cook at 100% power for 1 minute. Cut or pinch the tops off the snow peas and add to corn. Microwave for another minute.

Remove chicken packets from boiling water when done. Unwrap each breast and slice them crosswise into four pieces. Hold the breast with tongs to avoid burning your fingers.

Place a generous serving of mashed potato on warmed plates and top with chicken slices. Serve vegetables alongside. A knob of butter on top of the steaming corn is an attractive addition. If you really want to impress, see the Helpful Hints section for a quick and easy-to-make chicken gravy to drizzle over the top.

Wine suggestion: West Australian unwooded Chardonnay, Hunter Valley Verdelho.

Bachelor-Style Chicken Casserole

When the weather gets cooler, we all reach for the comfort food. It's also terrific when we mightn't be feeling on top of our game, like after a big weekend of socialising. This casserole is great comfort food and very easy to put together. Served in front of an open fire with a glass of your favourite wine, you'll have a very happy dinner guest!

Preparation time: 15 minutes   **Cooking time:** 60 minutes

Rating: or if served in front of fire:

This casserole is great comfort food and very easy to put together.

Ingredients

olive oil

1 large onion, chopped into medium pieces

1 red capsicum, chopped

1 stalk celery, chopped

1 carrot, chopped

6 mushrooms, chopped

1 tsp ground cumin

1/2 tsp ground chillies

1/2 cup medium or dry white wine

1 cooked chook, flesh only, meat pulled apart into small pieces

3 rashers of bacon, chopped

1 medium potato and 1 sweet potato or 2 medium potatoes, cut into small cubes and pre-cooked in microwave for 2 minutes on high

1 medium tin chickpeas

1 small tin red kidney beans

1 small tin corn kernels

1 packet of French onion soup (dry)

420 g tin of cream of chicken soup plus ½ tin of water

1/3 cup full cream

salt and pepper

1 cup uncooked rice, any style

2–4 sprigs, flat-leaf parsley

Method

Preheat oven to 200° C (or 180° if using convection/fan-forced oven).

Add olive oil to a medium fry pan over medium-high heat, and lightly fry the onion, capsicum, celery, carrots and mushrooms with the cumin and ground chillies, stirring well, for 5 minutes. Add the wine and simmer for 5 minutes.

In a large oven-safe dish, mix the pre-cooked potato, chicken pieces, bacon, chickpeas, kidney beans, corn, contents of French onion soup packet, cream of chicken soup and 1/2 soup can of water. Add the sautéed vegetables from the fry pan and mix well together.

Set dish in oven and cook for 40 minutes, stirring halfway through. Add cream, salt and pepper to taste, and cook for an additional 20 minutes.

Whilst the casserole is in the oven, place your rice in a medium saucepan covered with boiling water. Cook via absorption method (time will depend on your rice type so check the packet). Turn off once cooked and let sit, covered.

Serve casserole on warmed plates atop a bed of rice and garnish with some flat leaf parsley.

Wine suggestion: light red wine, such as Sangiovese or Shiraz/Viognier blend.

Tuna Pasta

This is another recipe that dates back to the days of my Clapham South flat. Three out of four of us in the flat used this recipe with success. The fourth flat mate never tried it, strangely enough. This is another terrific and simple dish, tasty and not in the least bit heavy. Plus, it doesn't take long to prepare, leaving you more time to devote to getting to know your guest on the couch instead of spending it in the kitchen.

Preparation time: 5–10 minutes   **Cooking time:** 20 minutes

Rating:

This is another terrific and simple dish, tasty and not in the least bit heavy.

Ingredients

1 medium brown onion, finely chopped

2 medium cloves garlic, crushed or finely chopped

salt and pepper

1 chilli, fresh or powdered (optional)

1/2 medium-sized red capsicum, finely chopped

3 mushrooms, finely chopped

20–30 capers, drained and roughly chopped

6 black olives, sliced

1/2 cup dry white wine

450 g tin tuna in spring water, drained

70 g tomato paste

250 g farfalle (bow tie-shaped pasta)

100 ml cream (pouring or thickened; your choice)

grated Parmesan cheese (optional)

cracked pepper

Method

Place onion and garlic in a bowl; and capsicum and capers in another. Keep mushrooms separate.

Set a medium fry pan (one that has a lid) over low heat and add a small splash of olive oil. Sauté onions and garlic, adding a dash of pepper and salt (and chilli, if desired). Once the onions turn slightly opaque, add 1/3 of the wine (1/6 cup) and stir. Increase heat to medium-low. Simmer gently.

Add capsicum and capers to fry pan; sauté for 1 minute. Add mushrooms and olives, along with another 1/3 (1/6 cup) of the wine.

Break up tuna with a fork in small bowl. Add a small amount at a time to pan, stirring, until all the tuna has been incorporated. Add tomato paste and mix in well. Add the remaining 1/3 (1/6 cup) of the wine. Stir and cook for 5 minutes, maintaining a gentle simmer.

Boil pasta in boiling salted water until *al dente*, according to package directions. (Texture should be slightly chewy and not too soft.) Drain, reserving 1/2 cup of pasta water for the sauce (to use if it looks too thick).

Meanwhile, add cream to the tuna mixture and stir, blending well. Simmer on low heat, covered for 3–5 minutes, stirring occasionally. (It should achieve a creamy tomato look by now.) Use some of the reserved pasta water if the sauce needs thinning.

Return drained pasta to saucepan. Mix 3 ladles of the tuna sauce into the pasta and stir to coat pasta. Pour pasta into warmed bowls and top with tuna sauce. Wipe any splatters off the rims of the bowls and serve with freshly grated Parmesan cheese and cracked pepper.

Wine suggestion: Pinot Noir

Chicken Parmigiana

Everyone loves a good Parmigiana, right? And there's no better one than a deliciously prepared, home-cooked Parmigiana. A recent trip down to Victoria reminded me how good this dish can be. They even have a website that rates them! The big tip is to prepare your own chicken fillet — don't get one of the processed ones. You'll reap the rewards for the effort!

Preparation time: 15 minutes   **Cooking time:** 30 minutes

Rating:

Everyone loves a good Parmigiana, right? And there's no better one than a deliciously prepared, home-cooked Parmigiana.

Ingredients

2 whole, plump chicken fillets

flour

eggs, lightly beaten

panko (Japanese-style) breadcrumbs

frozen chips/fries

butter

olive oil

2 cloves garlic, finely chopped

2 shallots, or 1 large brown onion, finely chopped

1/2 red capsicum, finely chopped

100 g mushrooms, finely chopped

cracked pepper

50 ml red wine (drinkable!)

400 ml prepared tomato sauce, such as Neapolitana

1/8 cup each, oregano and basil, finely chopped

2 thin slices ham

1/2 cup grated Parmesan cheese

1 cup grated mozzarella cheese

Method

Preheat your oven to 210° C.

Lay chicken breasts on cutting board and butterfly them by slicing them laterally so that they open like a book and sit flat. Place each chicken breast with the cut side down on some baking paper and, using a meat mallet, carefully flatten the chicken till even and about 1 cm thick.

Set up one plate of plain flour, one with the beaten egg and one with the breadcrumbs. Dust the chicken breast in the flour, shaking off any excess. Dip to coat in beaten egg and then dredge in breadcrumbs. Dip again in egg, coating completely and then cover with breadcrumbs a second time. (This double-coating gives an excellent crust.) Set aside on a plate and place covered in the fridge till you are ready to cook.

Prepare your frozen chips by spreading them onto an oven-proof tray and bake according to package directions. Keep an eye on them so they cook evenly on the tray.

Heat 1 tablespoon of butter with 1 tablespoon of olive oil in a medium saucepan over medium-low heat. Cook garlic and shallots (or onion), stirring frequently. As the onion starts to turn opaque, add the capsicum and then the mushrooms. Sprinkle a good amount of cracked pepper into the pan. Cook for 2 minutes and then add the red wine. After another couple of minutes, add the tomato sauce and the chopped herbs. Simmer for 20 minutes, stirring occasionally.

While the sauce is cooking, in a fry pan over medium heat (no higher or you'll burn the breadcrumbs), melt a small amount of butter with some olive oil. Cook chicken for 2 minutes on each side. You may need to add some more oil and/or butter as you turn them over, if the breadcrumbs have absorbed the initial amount (not too much or the breadcrumb crust will become too oily). Once cooked, place the chicken onto some baking paper set in an oven tray.

Combine Parmesan and mozzarella cheeses in a bowl. Place a slice of ham on top of the chicken, cover with several spoonfuls of the sauce and then top with a decent sprinkle of the mixed cheese. Bake for 10–15 minutes until the cheese starts to get a nice golden colour.

Plate up with chips and a fresh garden salad, with a nice dressing such as the one under Helpful Hints at the start of this book.

Drink suggestion: This is terrific with a lovely pale ale. A Pinot or Italian variety like a Nebbiolo or Tempranillo would also complement the Parmigiana very well.

Veal Scaloppine with Hazelnuts, Balsamic Vinegar and Hazelnut Liqueur

This recipe is pure gold, guaranteed to dazzle! It may sound complicated but, trust me, it is not. The veal melts in the mouth with a medley of beautiful flavours and the greens give it a nice balance. This is truly a meal for a really special evening. (Then again, isn't every dinner date special?)

Preparation time: 10 minutes   **Cooking time:** 30 minutes

Rating:

This recipe is pure gold, guaranteed to dazzle!

Ingredients

50 g dry-roasted hazelnuts

400 g veal scaloppine

1/2 cup plain flour

50 g butter, divided

1 tbsp vegetable oil

1/2 tbsp olive oil

1 cup dry white wine

salt and freshly ground black pepper

1 tbsp balsamic vinegar

30 ml hazelnut liqueur, such as Frangelico

½ packet (250g) of pappardelle pasta

trimmed green beans and broccolini

Method

Remove as much of the remaining hazelnut skins as possible by rubbing between your fingers or inside a clean dishtowel. Chop into small pieces, about the size of a grain of rice.

Cut veal into 5 to 8 cm-sized pieces and flatten with a meat mallet until about 5 mm thick and even. Spread flour onto a large, flat dish or, alternatively, put in a small plastic bag.

Boil pasta gently in salted water for 10 minutes. Remove from heat. Drain and return to saucepan, tossing gently with half a tablespoon of olive oil to coat. Cover.

Melt 30 grams of butter with the tablespoon of vegetable oil in a fry pan over high heat. When the pan is sufficiently hot, dredge the veal pieces into the flour (or shake them individually in the plastic bag), lightly covering each side and shaking any excess flour off. Don't be tempted to coat the pieces ahead of time, as the flour will get sodden. It should be done just before frying. Add veal pieces to fry pan, cooking in batches. Do not overcrowd the pan or it will be difficult to turn the pieces and you'll risk steaming the meat instead of browning it. Cook 1 minute or so on each side, until lightly browned. Be careful not to overcook or they'll get tough! Remove and keep warm. Continue the process till all the veal is browned.

Place the hazelnut liqueur in a small saucepan and heat over medium-low heat until nearly simmering. Lower heat and cover.

Without cleaning the fry pan used to brown the veal, add the white wine and deglaze over medium heat, scraping up any browned bits. Add most of the chopped hazelnuts (leave a small amount to use as garnish at the end) and simmer until nearly evaporated. Stir in the remaining 20 grams of butter.

Whilst the wine is reducing, place the beans and broccolini into a microwave-safe dish and cook on high for 2 minutes. Alternatively, place them into a hot wok and stir-fry in 2 teaspoons of vegetable oil for 60–90 seconds. Keep warm.

Sprinkle the scaloppine with salt and pepper and return to the pan. Pour any juice remaining on the plate in the pan as well. Keeping the heat on medium, turn the scaloppine several times to coat well in the sauce for 2 to 3 minutes at most.

Add the warmed hazelnut liqueur to the pan and ignite. The easiest way to do this is to carefully wave a lit match at the pan's edge just above the contents to ignite the fumes.

Turn off the heat. Pour the balsamic vinegar over the scaloppine and turn again to coat well.

Place a few pieces of the pappardelle pasta onto each warmed plate. Cover with some of the green beans and broccolini and then top with a generous amount of veal scaloppine and the sauce. Sprinkle the remaining chopped hazelnuts on top. Serve.

Wine suggestion: Margaret River Cabernet-Merlot.

Pizza

Pizza is incredibly versatile. It can be served as either a starter or the main course. You can serve it at lunch, mid-afternoon, in the evening or even once you get home after a late night out. The mark of a great pizza is to keep the crust thin and don't go overboard on the toppings. Otherwise, you'll end up with a half-cooked, soggy pizza that's so busy that all the tastes blur together. That goes for the cheese, too. Go easy on it.

I use thin bases — Bazaar™ brand crusts are good (from Coles). Or you can make your own (great, but time consuming). A pizza stone comes in handy to really crisp up the crust.

I've included two types of pizza that I have had success with. By all means, feel free to experiment, again, going light on the topping quantities. (If you come up with a real pants dropper, then drop me a line and let me know. I just might include it in my next cookbook!)

I recommend serving these with a nice glass of Sangiovese or Tempranillo — they are great, light, Italian red wines that go with pizza. Alternatively, a good cold beer goes a treat. Good pizza is always a hit. Don't be shy to try your hand at them.

Potato, Rosemary and Chorizo Pizza

Preparation time: 10-15 minutes   **Cooking time:** 10-15 minutes

Rating:

Ingredients

1 pizza dough crust

equal parts tomato sauce and barbecue sauce, amount determined by crust size

2 large potatoes, thinly sliced 2 mm thick, oiled on both sides

olive oil

4 sprigs of rosemary, each 10 cm long, with leaves stripped and chopped finely and stems discarded

salt and pepper

1 Spanish chorizo sausage, thinly sliced (chopped bacon or thinly sliced pepperoni can be substituted)

1/2 cup freshly grated Parmesan cheese

Good pizza is always
a hit. Don't be shy to
try your hand at them.

Method

Preheat oven to 220° C, with your pizza stone or tray inside.

Place pizza dough on tray and cover lightly and evenly with tomato-barbecue mix. Cover up to the edges.

Place potato slices on top of pizza sauce, covering fully and overlapping slightly. Sprinkle evenly with chopped rosemary and salt/pepper. Bake 8–10 minutes.

Remove pizza from oven and arrange chorizo on top. Lightly sprinkle with Parmesan. Return to oven and bake for 5 minutes. Remove, cut into slices, keeping pizza intact to serve at the table.

Wine suggestion: Sangiovese or Sangiovese/Cabernet Sauvignon blend, such as Chapel Hill Il Vescovo

Ham and Spinach Pizza with Pine Nuts and Sultanas on a Pesto Crust

Preparation time: 10–15 minutes   **Cooking time:** 10–15 minutes

Rating:

The mark of a great pizza is to keep the crust thin and don't go overboard on the toppings.

Ingredients

1 pizza dough base

150 g bag of baby spinach, washed

small knob butter

juice of 1/4 lemon

cracked pepper

prepared basil pesto (any brand)

1/4 cup pignolis (pine nuts)

1/4 cup sultanas

100 g leg ham, chopped

grated Parmesan or mozzarella cheese

Method

Preheat oven to 220° C, with your pizza stone or tray inside.

Meanwhile, melt butter in small fry pan over medium heat. Add 3/4 of the bag of baby spinach, squeezing lemon juice over spinach and adding cracked pepper to taste. Cook until spinach wilts, 1 to 2 minutes.

Place pizza dough on preheated tray or stone and cover dough with a thin, even layer of pesto. Layer the wilted spinach on the pesto and sprinkle with cheese. Add chopped ham and pine nuts.

Bake for 6 minutes.

Remove from oven. Sprinkle the sultanas, a little more cheese and remaining raw spinach leaves over the top and bake an additional 5 minutes. Remove from oven, cut into slices and serve whole at the table.

Wine suggestion: Margaret River Tempranillo

Salmon Patties

Salmon patties are a great idea for a summer lunch or dinner. Both light and healthy, they score big with the health/fitness-conscious date. There are enough patties made with this recipe that you could serve them for lunch, go off and have some fun and then have more for dinner that evening, if you're so inclined!

Preparation time: 90 minutes   **Cooking time:** 5 minutes

Rating:

Salmon patties
are a great idea for
a summer lunch or
dinner.

Ingredients

3/8 cup of capers, chopped, divided into 1/8 of a cup and 2/8 of a cup

50 ml mayonnaise

1 gherkin, finely chopped

8 sprigs of fresh parsley, chopped, divided

3 small chilli, such as Birdseye, deseeded, chopped, divided into 2 for patties and 1 for the sauce

500 g potatoes peeled and cut into 3 cm pieces

1 tbsp butter

1/2 tsp ground nutmeg

2 small spring onions

1/4 cup of chopped fresh dill

415 g tin of red salmon

100 g smoked salmon, chopped

3 eggs

1 cup breadcrumbs

1 cup flour

olive oil

tossed green salad as accompaniment

Method

To make the sauce, chop 1/8 cup (about 12-15) capers. Mix with mayonnaise, chopped gherkin, 2 sprigs of chopped parsley and 1 small chilli. Set aside.

Cover potatoes with water in medium saucepan and bring to boil over medium-high heat. Salt the water and boil potatoes for 15–20 minutes, until tender enough to pierce easily with a fork. Mash with butter and ground nutmeg. Set aside to cool completely. (If you're short for time, chill them for 15-20 minutes in the refrigerator.)

Combine spring onions, dill, remaining capers, parsley and chilli in a medium-sized bowl. Add the red salmon, smoked salmon and 1 egg, mixing well. Add the cooled mashed potatoes and mix well.

Form into 6 to 8 patties.

Lightly beat the remaining 2 eggs in a bowl. Set out two small plates, one on either side of the bowl containing the egg. Place 1/4 cup of flour on one plate and 1/4 cup of breadcrumbs on another. Dip each patty into the flour to coat, and set on a tray, replenishing flour and breadcrumbs in dishes as needed. Refrigerate patties for at least 1 hour (otherwise, they will fall apart during cooking).

Heat some olive oil in a large fry pan over medium heat. When hot, fry patties in batches until golden brown on both sides.

To serve, place 2 patties on a warm plate with a dollop of sauce on the side. Serve with salad.

Wine suggestion: a well chilled dry Riesling or West Australian Semillon/Sauvignon Blanc blend

Balsamic Beef Rib

Now, we all know that blokes love meat on their plates. So, how do you cook up a nice slab of meat and impress your guest just as much? This whole rib goes beautifully as a Sunday lunch, served on a bed of leafy greens and accompanied with a lovely Shiraz. It's also great for dinner any other day or cold for the next day's lunch.

Preparation time: 2–3 hours   **Cooking time:** 60 minutes

Rating:

It's also great for dinner any other day or cold for the next day's lunch.

Ingredients

4 garlic cloves, chopped

1 cup olive oil

1 cup (250 ml) good quality balsamic vinegar

zest of 1 lemon (yellow rind only; no white pith!)

6 basil leaves, chopped

1 to 1.2 kg whole rib piece (ask your butcher to trim it up nicely)

120 g bag of rocket and spinach leaf mixed greens, rinsed and drained well

1 medium red onion, sliced finely

Method

In a small bowl, mix together the chopped garlic, olive oil, balsamic vinegar, lemon zest and basil leaves.

Score the beef rib by placing a couple of shallow slits down each edge of the piece, especially through any connective tissue. This will allow the marinade to soak into the meat well.

Set the beef rib into a baking dish and pour the marinade over. Turn the meat several times to coat completely. Cover with plastic wrap and place in the fridge for 2 to 3 hours, turning meat every hour.

Preheat oven to 200° C about 20 minutes before beef comes out of the refrigerator.

Heat up the barbecue or hotplate on your stove. Lower heat to medium and grill each side of the rib for 2 to 3 minutes, taking care that any excess oil doesn't drip and flame up on the barbecue. This should take about 10–12 minutes total. Brush on some more of the marinade and then place beef back in baking dish. Cook in the oven for 30 minutes for medium-rare.

Remove beef from oven and cover with aluminium foil to rest for 20 minutes. (It will continue to cook a little with the residual heat whilst resting, becoming nice and tender as the meat relaxes.)

Arrange the leafy greens on a large serving plate and arrange the sliced onion attractively around the edges. Carve the rib into thin slices and place in the centre, on top of the greens. Drizzle with any meat juices that remain.

Place platter onto the table so your guest (or guests!) can help themselves. I guarantee they're going to want seconds!

Wine suggestion: Barossa Shiraz

Sesame Rice with Haloumi and Steamed Vegetables

There are few queries that instil fear in a bachelor more than, "How many other girls have you slept with?" or "How about we go over to my parents' place for dinner?" One other that can make your heart sink, is "Thanks, I'd love to come over for dinner. It's not a problem that I'm a vegetarian, is it?"

If you're lucky, she'll eat chicken or, better yet, fish. But, just in case, here's a terrific dish guaranteed to please the most stringent of vegetarians. I actually like haloumi myself. The marinade is a real treat, especially drizzled over the veggies. She'll surely be impressed that you are happy eating a meal without meat. Hope it works and makes the best out of a dire situation. My advice, if she's a diehard vegetarian and you're not — it's probably not a match made in heaven, even if this dish is!

Preparation time: 10 minutes plus 1 hour marinating time   **Cooking time:** 40 minutes

Rating:

...here's a terrific dish guaranteed to please the most stringent of vegetarians.

Ingredients

4 tbsp lime juice

30 ml sesame oil

50 ml sweet chilli sauce

black pepper

2 180 g packets of haloumi, cut into 1 cm slices

1 cup brown rice

4 tbsp sesame seeds

1/2 tsp sea salt

400–500 g mixed seasonal veggies, such as capsicum, snow peas, zucchini, carrots and mushrooms

Method

Combine lime juice, sesame oil, sweet chilli sauce and ground black pepper. Pour over sliced haloumi. Cover and refrigerate for 1 hour.

Rinse the rice, then cover with water in a saucepan (that has a lid) and bring to the boil. Reduce to a simmer, cover and cook for 30 minutes. If not finished cooking, continue simmering covered for another 5 to 10 minutes. Drain any residual water and then rinse with boiling water.

Meanwhile, place the sesame seeds in a small, dry fry pan and toast over medium-high heat, tossing or stirring frequently, for several minutes until golden. Place in a mortar with the sea salt and grind together with the pestle. (If you haven't a mortar and pestle, a bowl and a blunt object such as a thick wooden handle will do.) Stir sesame-salt mixture into rice.

Take the haloumi out of the bowl, letting any excess marinade drain off and cook in a non-stick fry pan over medium heat for about 2 minutes each side, until golden brown. Be careful not to scorch! Place the fried haloumi on some paper towels to drain.

Whilst the haloumi is cooking, place your seasonal vegetable selection in a steamer. Alternatively, use a microwave-safe dish and cook in the microwave at 100% power for 3–4 minutes. If some of your veggies are harder than others, cook them for 2 minutes first, adding the rest and continuing to cook for 1 or more minutes.

Serve strips of haloumi atop a bed of rice, with the vegetables alongside. Drizzle some of the remaining haloumi marinade over the top of the veggies and haloumi.

Wine suggestion: Pinot Gris

Seafood Pie

This is a lovely version of a seafood shepherd's pie. With the plethora of terrific seafood in Australia these days, try combining some with fresh vegetables in a white wine sauce, topped with mashed potatoes to create a simple yet beautiful meal. Serve this up to a hungry dinner guest and the compliments will flow as generously as the wine!

Preparation time: 40 minutes   **Cooking time:** 25 minutes

Rating:

*Serve this up to a
hungry dinner guest and
the compliments will
flow as generously as
the wine!*

Ingredients

4 medium potatoes, peeled and cut into 5 cm pieces

2 tbsp butter

2 tbsp milk

4 eggs

white vinegar

1 large fish fillet with firm, white flesh such as barramundi, bass or cod

12 mussels, shells removed

6 medium green prawns, peeled and de-veined

6 scallops, shells removed

1 medium onion, minced

1 medium carrot, peeled and diced

1 stick of celery, minced

120 g fresh spinach or chopped silverbeet

1/2 cup dry, white wine

2 tbsp Dijon, wholegrain or English mustard

200 ml full cream

flat leaf parsley, chopped (optional)

Method

Place potato pieces in a saucepan of cold water. Bring to boil, uncovered, over high heat; boil for 15–20 minutes, until tender. Drain. Add butter and milk; mash till smooth. Set aside.

In a separate saucepan, cover eggs with water, add splash of white vinegar and bring to a boil. When water begins to boil, remove from heat and cover. Let sit 10 minutes. Drain and cool under cold water. Set aside.

Pre-heat oven to 200° C.

On a clean cutting board, cut fish fillet into bite-sized pieces, removing any bones that remain. Cut your prawns into halves, lengthwise. Leave mussels and scallops whole.

Heat 1 tablespoon olive oil in fry pan over medium heat. Lightly sauté the onion for 1 minute. Add carrot, followed by celery and cook for 5 minutes. Add the white wine, stirring for 1 minute; then add the cream. Reduce heat to low and cook for 3 minutes. Add the spinach/silverbeet and cook for another 2 minutes, until wilted.

Toss the seafood and mustard in an oven-proof, 24 cm diameter casserole dish until well-coated. Mix in vegetables, along with some salt and freshly ground pepper. Toss gently until combined, smoothing out the top.

Peel eggs and cut into quarters. Lay the egg pieces on top of the seafood mixture. Cover completely with a layer of mashed potato, being careful not to crush the eggs. Lightly brush the top with melted butter or place a couple of dobs of butter over, to help brown the top.

Place the dish, uncovered, on top of a baking sheet to prevent spills. Bake for 20–25 minutes. Remove from oven and slide a skewer into the centre of the pie to test if it is done. If the skewer is not hot enough, bake again at 5-minute intervals until hot enough to serve.

Serve on warmed plates, decorated with sprigs of parsley.

Wine suggestion: Eden Valley Riesling or W.A. Semillon/Sauvignon Blanc blend

Lights Out Leg of Lamb

Have the lights just gone out? Never let a lack of electricity affect your romantic plans. The barbecue is a bachelor's best friend when it comes to producing a very impressive meal for a dinner guest. And the advantage of no power is that you will need to use multiple candles around the dinner table and house — and we all know that girls are a sucker for candles! So, fire up the barbecue as this boned leg of lamb is a sure winner.

Preparation time: 1 hour (best to leave marinating longer if possible)
Cooking time: 30 minutes

Rating:

Ingredients

1 butterflied leg of lamb, boned (by either you or your butcher)

2 tbsp olive oil

4 tbsp soy sauce

2 tbsp Dijon mustard

3 cloves garlic, finely chopped

4 sprigs of rosemary, woody stems removed, leaves finely chopped

The barbecue is a bachelor's best friend when it comes to producing a very impressive meal for a dinner guest.

Method

Score the lamb leg on the fat covering side with a sharp knife, making ½ cm slits (small cuts into the fat so that the marinade can soak into the meat).

Mix the olive oil, soy sauce and Dijon mustard in a small bowl. Combine garlic and rosemary and spread over both sides of the lamb. Pour oil/soy sauce/mustard mixture, coating both sides. Cover and let marinate for at least 30 minutes at room temperature.

If, in fact, your electricity is on, preheat oven to 200° C (180° if using a convection/fan-forced oven).

Now, turn on the barbecue, clean the grill section and preheat on high. Once hot, lower heat to medium and place the butterflied lamb leg onto the grill, cooking each side for 5 minutes. (Note: when cooking fat side down, be alert for flame-ups caused by drips; you do not want the lamb cooking in direct flame.)

Transfer lamb to tray. Cook lamb on tray either in oven for 20 minutes or, alternatively, turn off all but one burner on the barbecue and place lamb tray on far end, not over direct heat. Close barbecue lid and keep a careful eye on the barbecue's internal temperature to ensure it is not getting too hot. Aim for 200-220 ºC as the correct temperature.

Remove lamb from oven or barbecue, cover with aluminium foil and let rest for 5 minutes. Carve. Serve with your favourite salad or even a jacket potato done in foil on the barbecue (these will take 20–30 minutes to do).

Wine suggestion: Coonawarra Cabernet Sauvignon

Barbecue White Reef Fish Fillets with Asian Sauce

We are very lucky in Australia to have such a wide and delicious variety of fabulous fresh fish. I first tasted this dish at a friend's barbecue and loved it — the combination of the lovely sweet flesh of the fish with the hot, sweet and spicy tastes of the sauce were a marriage made in heaven. This might be just the dish to serve that special someone on a night you hope to get closer (a lot closer!) The heat of the sauce will melt away any inhibitions. A glass or two of white wine wouldn't hurt, either!

Preparation time: 30 minutes   **Cooking time:** 5–6 minutes

Rating:

We are very lucky in Australia to have such a wide and delicious variety of fabulous fresh fish.

Ingredients

2 large Red Emperor fillets (or similar white reef fish)

prepared basil pesto

1 lemon, zested

olive oil

4 tbsp soy sauce

2 tsp fish sauce

3 cm piece of ginger, minced

1 clove garlic, minced

2 tbsp rice wine vinegar

1 tbsp brown sugar

1/3 cup fish stock

1 chilli, seeded and chopped finely

1 tbsp olive oil

2 baking potatoes

sour cream or butter for topping

Method

Coat the fish with the pesto and lemon zest and chill, covered, for 30 minutes.

Preheat barbecue to high.

Cook the potatoes for 3 minutes in the microwave on 100% power. Remove from oven and wrap in aluminium foil and then place on barbecue for 10 minutes, turning regularly. Remove and keep warm.

In a bowl or jug, combine soy sauce, fish sauce, fish stock, rice wine vinegar and brown sugar; stir until well blended. Set aside.

Heat olive oil in a fry pan over medium heat. Sauté the ginger, garlic and chilli for 1 minute. Add soy sauce mixture, increase heat and bring to a boil. Lower heat and simmer.

Lightly oil a sheet of aluminium foil and place it on the barbecue. Turn heat down to medium, and place the fish on the foil and cook for 90 seconds to 2 minutes on each side, depending on the thickness of the fish fillet, until just opaque. Be careful not to overcook or fish will dry out.

Serve fish with several spoonfuls of sauce drizzled over.

Serve with baked potato topped with butter or sour cream and a fresh garden salad of lettuce, cherry tomatoes, cucumber and crumbled feta cheese. A crispy Asian noodle salad would also work well here, such as the one listed on the packet of Chang's™ original fried noodles.

Wine suggestion: Tasmanian Sauvignon Blanc.

Chicken Korma

Now, I know what you're thinking — cooking a curry from scratch is hard work! Well, let me tell you, it isn't that hard. It requires a blender and a selection of spices, but they keep well in air-tight jars and should last a year or so if kept away from heat and bright light. This curry uses readily available spices, is quite mild so you won't scare off your guest, and I guarantee it is well worth the effort. The best thing is that it actually benefits from having been made a day before, so that the taste can really develop, leaving you free to focus solely on entertaining your guest. You'll love it, and your guest is sure to be impressed, especially if you leave the spice jars sitting next to the stove to prove that you really did make this yourself!

Preparation time: 20 minutes   **Cooking time:** 60 minutes

Rating:

Ingredients

2 onions, 1 thinly sliced, 1 roughly chopped

4 garlic cloves, peeled and halved

3 cm piece fresh ginger, chopped (Note: ginger is actually easiest to peel with a spoon!)

1/3 cup raw cashews

2 large chillies, deseeded (preferably dried, to increase the heat), or 1 tsp ground chilli powder

3/4 cup (190 ml) water

2 tsp ground coriander

1 tsp ground cumin

1/4 tsp each of ground cinnamon, cardamom, nutmeg and cloves

1/2 tsp saffron strands, crushed and dissolved in 2 tbsp boiling water

3 tbsp vegetable oil

2 tsp salt

750 g of boneless chicken pieces, cut into small cubes

3 fully ripe tomatoes, deseeded and pureed

125 ml natural (plain) yoghurt

125 ml full or cooking cream

1 tbsp coriander, chopped

The best thing is that it actually benefits from having been made a day before, so that the taste can really develop, leaving you free to focus solely on entertaining your guest.

Method

To make the korma paste, place the thinly sliced onion in a bowl and set aside. Place the chopped onion, halved garlic cloves, ginger and cashews in the blender. Blend for 10 seconds; and then add 1/2 cup (125 ml) of water. Blend until smooth. Add coriander, cumin, cinnamon, cardamom, nutmeg and cloves; blend. Add saffron and blend.

Heat 3 tablespoons of vegetable oil in a large saucepan over medium heat. Add the thinly sliced onion and sauté for at least 5 minutes, until onion slices are soft and slightly transparent. Add the korma paste. Rinse out the blender with the remaining 1/4 cup of water and add to the saucepan along with the salt. Stir frequently, for 15–20 minutes, until it reaches the consistency of runny peanut butter.

Add chicken cubes and combine, ensuring all the pieces are well covered with the paste. Add pureed tomatoes. Lower heat to medium-low. Cover saucepan and let cook for 20 minutes. Add the plain yoghurt and cream to the saucepan and mix well. Stir in the coriander and continue to simmer for 20–40 minutes. Set aside to cool slightly. Taste and season, as required.

Like all curries, this is best served the following day. Re-heat and serve on a bed of basmati rice, garnished with fresh coriander and a side plate of poppadums. But, if you can't make it ahead of time, go ahead and eat it straight away. It'll still taste great!

Beverage suggestion: Singa or Tiger beer

Lamb and Yoghurt Pasta Bake

This is a great pasta bake, with lots of veggies. The unusual topping of Greek yoghurt really complements the lamb and eggplant. There is sure to be one impressed guest when this is served at your dinner table. Serves 6, as you know how we all love leftovers!

Preparation time: 60 minutes   **Cooking time:** 30 minutes

Rating:

This is a great pasta bake,
with lots of veggies.

Ingredients

250 g dried penne pasta

1 large eggplant, trimmed and sliced thinly into about 20 slices

olive oil for frying

750 g lamb mince

2 cloves garlic, minced

1 brown onion, coarsely chopped

1 medium carrot, peeled and diced

1 medium zucchini, grated

400 g tin of crushed tomatoes

1-1/2 tbsp tomato paste

1 chicken stock cube, crushed

2 tbsp each of chopped fresh oregano and rosemary

250 g Greek yoghurt

1 egg, lightly beaten

1/4 cup breadcrumbs

1/4 cup mixture of shredded Parmesan and cheddar cheeses

Method

Pre-heat oven to 180° C.

Cook pasta in salted, boiling water according to package directions; drain and set aside.

Brush or spray each eggplant slice on both sides with olive oil. Heat a non-stick fry pan over medium-high heat and cook eggplant slices for 2 minutes on each side till light brown. Transfer to a plate and set aside. Alternatively use a flat toasted sandwich maker and cook multiple slices of eggplant at once.

Heat 1 tablespoon olive oil in the same pan over medium-high heat. Brown lamb mince with garlic, stirring frequently with a wooden spoon to break up any lumps. Add a good dose of salt and freshly ground pepper and the chopped rosemary. When mince is thoroughly cooked and nicely browned, transfer to a large saucepan.

Heat 1/2 tablespoon olive oil in fry pan over medium-low heat. Add the chopped onion and gently sauté until the onion softens. Add the carrot and zucchini. Fry for 3 minutes. Remove from heat and add to mince mixture.

Heat mince mixture over medium heat, adding tomatoes, tomato paste and crushed stock cube. Cook, stirring occasionally, for 3 to 5 minutes. Turn off heat; add chopped oregano and rosemary, followed by the cooked pasta. Mix well.

In a deep 25 cm x 25 cm ovenproof baking dish, cover bottom with 1/3 of the eggplant slices in a single layer, slightly overlapping. Top with half the mince and pasta mix, then 1/3 of the eggplant in a single layer, with the slices slightly overlapping. Top with the remaining mince mixture and cover with the remaining 1/3 of the eggplant slices, again in a single layer, slightly overlapping.

Whisk together the Greek yoghurt and lightly beaten egg in a bowl. Spread it over the eggplant. Mix the breadcrumbs and cheeses together and sprinkle over the yoghurt. Bake for 30 minutes.

Serve with a Greek salad or steamed green vegetables.

Wine suggestion: Cabernet Sauvignon or Cabernet-Merlot blend.

Nathan's Slow-Cooked Mediterranean Chicken

Slow cookers (or crock pots, as I knew them back in the day) are an essential part of the modern day kitchen. With many of us 'time-poor', they are extremely helpful. And there is no one who doesn't like coming home to the smell of some home cooking. Slow cookers do it all (well, nearly all).

This dish was inspired by one of my good bachelor mates, who has found out how good it is to cook meals to impress. Well done, Nathan! Start this at least 4-1/2 hours before serving.

Preparation time: 20 minutes   **Cooking time:** 4–8 hours

Rating:

And there is no one who doesn't like coming home to the smell of some home cooking.

Ingredients

500 g chicken thighs, boned and chopped into bite-sized pieces

4 medium potatoes, peeled and cubed

1 brown onion, roughly chopped

1 red capsicum, roughly chopped

400 g tin crushed tomatoes

140 g tomato paste (1 small tub)

2 tbsp brown sugar

1 tbsp each chopped fresh thyme and oregano

salt and cracked black pepper

1/2 cup white wine

1/2 cup chicken stock

1 chorizo sausage, sliced finely

12 black olives, roughly chopped

1 cup medium grain brown rice

2 tsp cornflour dissolved in 2 tbsp water

several sprigs of flat leaf parsley

Method

Place the chicken, potatoes, onion, capsicum, crushed tomatoes, tomato paste, brown sugar, chopped herbs and salt and pepper into the slow cooker. Add the white wine and chicken stock. Stir well.

Turn the slow cooker onto high for 3 hours or set it on low if you are happy for it to take all day.

After 3 hours (or when you get home!), slice up the chorizo and olives and add to the slow cooker. Cook for a further hour on low heat, or 30 minutes on high.

Cover rice with boiling water in a small saucepan over low heat, so that the water level is about a centimetre higher than the rice; cover (read the pack for the 'absorption method'). The brown rice should take about 25–30 minutes.

Check the chicken. The sauce will be quite thin still. Add dissolved cornflour to the slow cooker and stir through. This will help thicken it up nicely. Taste; add salt and pepper as needed.

Once the rice is ready, serve into a bowl. Top with a good serving of the chicken and garnish with a small amount of flat leaf parsley.

Wine suggestion: Unwooded Chardonnay for white wine lovers, a lovely, earthy Grenache for the red drinkers.

Smoked Salmon and Baby Peas with Pasta

This is a little cracker of a dish. It's very tasty, but so light that you'll feel up to a little exertion after dinner. I threw this together one night, completely impromptu, in London, based on what I happened to have left in the fridge at the time. Even I was impressed and the evening quickly became a huge success, if I say so myself. I hope it works as well for you!

Preparation time: 5 minutes **Cooking time:** 15 minutes

Rating:

*This is a little cracker
of a dish.*

Ingredients

1 tbsp butter

1/4 red onion, finely chopped

1/2 cup frozen baby peas (not necessary to thaw first)

salt and pepper

juice of 1/4 lemon, pits removed

150 ml full cream

100 g smoked salmon, snipped into small pieces (kitchen scissors are great for this!)

200–250 g fettuccine pasta

Method

In a medium saucepan, put on water to boil for the pasta. Add a teaspoon of salt after it comes to a boil.

Meanwhile, melt butter in a small fry pan over low heat. Sauté red onion until opaque. You don't want the onions to colour. Add the frozen peas and stir for 2 minutes. Add some salt and cracked pepper to taste.

Increase heat to medium. Add lemon juice and stir for 30 seconds. Add the cream and bring to a gentle simmer for 10 to 12 minutes. Sauce will thicken as it cooks.

Boil pasta until *al dente*, according to package directions, stirring occasionally to prevent sticking together. Drain and then return to saucepan.

Sprinkle the salmon onto the pasta and stir through well. The heat of the pasta will cook the smoked salmon, turning it slightly opaque. Add the cream sauce and stir so all the pasta is nicely coated with the sauce.

Serve into warm bowls or onto plates. Trust me your dinner guest will be impressed!

Wine suggestion: Eden Valley Riesling or Pinot Gris

Desserts

Apple Turnovers (or as I like to call them Puff Pastry Pants Pleasers)

These are a great home-style dessert favourite. Light, healthy and tasty, these apple turnovers provide a great finish to any meal. And they are incredibly easy to make!

Preparation time: 25 minutes   **Cooking time:** 15 minutes

Rating:

These are a great home-style dessert favourite.

Ingredients

1 tbsp water

1 Granny Smith apple, peeled, quartered and sliced thinly

2 tbsp sultanas (optional)

1-1/2 tbsp brown sugar

1/4 tsp ground cinnamon

1 sheet puff pastry, thawed

1 egg, lightly beaten

Method

Preheat oven to 180° C (160° C if using convection/fan-forced oven).

In a small saucepan, heat the water, sliced apple, sultanas, brown sugar and cinnamon, and bring to a gentle boil. Simmer for 15 to 20 minutes until nearly all the liquid is gone. Cool.

Cut your pastry sheet into quarters. Place 1/4 of the apple mixture in the centre of each pastry. Fold the pastry over the mix, pressing the edges to seal. Roll the sealed edge of the pastry up and over itself and press down to seal completely. Do the same on each end, crimping to seal the parcel. Place each parcel on a baking tray and brush tops lightly and evenly with egg.

Bake for 15 minutes or until light brown. Serve with cream or ice cream.

No-Bake Lemon Cheesecake

I'm not sure why cheesecake went out of favour in restaurants. Most people I know still have a huge soft spot for cheesecake, whether baked or simply chilled like this one is. Since it is best made a day ahead and doesn't need to be baked, this is dead easy to make and even easier to eat. Probably a better dessert for the warmer months, as it's served cold.

Preparation time: 25 minutes   **Setting time:** additional 6 hours minimum

Rating:

Ingredients

500 g Philadelphia cream cheese
395 g tin condensed milk
1 lemon, zested and juiced

250 g packet of Scotch Finger biscuits*
150 g butter*

*Most people I know still
have a huge soft spot
for cheesecake, whether
baked or simply chilled
like this one is.*

Method

Crush the biscuits, either in a plastic bag with a rolling pin or meat mallet, or in a food processor.

Melt the butter gently in the microwave for 30 seconds on medium-high and mix in well with the crushed biscuits. Press evenly to cover the bottom of a 22 cm cake tin. (Springform types are best, so you can remove the sides easily.) Place baking pan into the freezer.

While the cookie crust is setting, cut cream cheese into 12 pieces. Place in a microwave-safe bowl and warm on low power for 30 seconds to soften. In a large mixing bowl, mix cream cheese with condensed milk using a handheld mixer for about 2 minutes till smooth. Add lemon zest and juice, beating for another minute until completely blended.

Remove baking pan from freezer and pour in cheese mixture. Smooth it out nicely so that you have a nice, even top. The cheesecake now needs to set either overnight in the refrigerator or, if serving same day, 2 hours in the freezer followed by *at least* 4 hours in the refrigerator.

To serve, remove the sides of the baking pan carefully. You may need to run a skewer or small knife around the outside first. Slice and serve on a dessert plate, and garnish with a sliced strawberry, some lemon zest curls or simply a dob of whipped cream.

*If you prefer a cookie crust up the sides as well as on the bottom, increase the amount of butter and cookies proportionately and press up the sides of springform pan before freezing.

Panna Cotta

What a lovely little dessert this is! My Italian mate, big George, swears by this traditional Italian dessert. I have to say, it is pretty much foolproof. Light and sweet, it is a perfect finish to any meal. It also looks pretty impressive!

Preparation time: 15 minutes   **Setting time:** 4 hours or more

Rating:

Ingredients

1 vanilla pod

1 cup (250 ml) milk

1 cup (250 ml) full cream

5 tbsp caster sugar

2 tsp powdered gelatine

2 tbsp cold water

*Light and sweet,
it is a perfect finish
to any meal.*

Method

Slice the vanilla pod down the middle and carefully scrape out all of the fine seeds into a small saucepan. (You can cut the pod into pieces before halving lengthwise and scraping them, if that is easier.) Over medium heat, bring seeds, vanilla pod pieces, milk, cream and caster sugar to the boil, stirring occasionally. Lower heat slightly and gently simmer for 5 minutes. Remove from heat.

While the cream is simmering, put the 2 tablespoons of cold water in a separate, small saucepan. Sprinkle the gelatine powder over the water and let sit for 5 minutes until set.

Remove the vanilla pod pieces from the cream. Gently dissolve the gelatine over low heat until it becomes a clear, thick liquid. Pour gelatine into the cream and mix well.

Divide mixture evenly between four small, round ramekins with straight sides (dariole moulds, those small metal containers that are used for baking individual pastries, are perfect) and refrigerate for at least 4 hours. To test for readiness, give the ramekin or mould a little shake — the mixture should be jelly-like in its movement, with only a slight wobble, like fully set custard.

To serve, dip the glasses into a bowl of warm water, being careful not to get water on the panna cotta. Invert a dessert plate atop the ramekin, turn over and gently shake the panna cotta until it releases onto the plate. If it doesn't release, carefully run a thin knife or skewer around the inside of the ramekin to loosen, trying not to cut into the panna cotta's edges and invert again. You will be left with a lovely, wobbly, white dessert with small black flecks from the vanilla seeds. This one needs no accompaniment. Serve it by itself and watch the smile spread across your special guest's face!

Chocolate Self-Saucing Puddings

These are decadent, rich and lovely! All you could ask for in a pudding. Just make sure you haven't eaten too much beforehand. This dish needs space! Makes 3.

Preparation time: 20–25 minutes   **Cooking time:** 15 minutes

Rating:

Ingredients

175 g dark cooking chocolate

2 eggs

1/2 tsp vanilla essence

1/6 cup plain flour

1/3 cup caster sugar

25 g butter, plus extra to grease ramekins

1 tsp icing sugar

*These are decadent,
rich and lovely!*

Method

Grease three 9 cm ramekins that are 5 cm deep, using a buttered paper towel. Cut rounds of baking paper by tracing around the bottom of each ramekin, and fit one inside the base of each ramekin. This will stop your pudding from staying in the dish when you try to turn it out onto the serving plate!

Cream the butter and sugar. (This means use your electric beaters to beat the two together until the butter turns pale and the sugar has been incorporated thoroughly.)

Break up the chocolate into small pieces and place in a microwave-safe bowl. In 30-second increments on medium (50%) power, heat the chocolate, stirring after each 30 seconds, until it all melts. Set aside.

Into the creamed butter and sugar, beat in the eggs one at a time with a wooden spoon. Add the vanilla, followed by the flour, mixing well. Add the melted chocolate to the mixture, and blend well. Divide the mixture equally between three ramekins, filling each about 2/3 full. Chill in the fridge until needed.

Pre-heat the oven to 200° C (180° C if using a convection oven). Remove ramekins from refrigerator and bake 12–15 minutes, until set without being too soft on top; it should have a nice crust. Cool for 5 minutes. Run a small knife around the edge of one of the puddings, top with a small, inverted plate and turn upside down. If the pudding hasn't set sufficiently and, instead collapses, return the remaining two to the oven for a further 3 minutes and then try again. This is why we have made 3 and not 2!

Now, take your serving plate, invert it and place it on top of the pudding and carefully turn it over so the crusty top is facing upwards. Gently shake the icing sugar through a fine sieve or wire mesh and dust the top of the puddings. Serve with a scoop of ice cream.

Congratulations! Your gorgeous pudding has a nice, firm exterior crust and a molten, creamy, chocolate filling within, that oozes out in a puddle when pressed. Guaranteed to melt away any resistance!

Pants Off Salmon — Recipes to Impress
Alec Bragg

Published by JoJo Publishing
First published 2012

'Yarra's Edge'
2203/80 Lorimer Street
Docklands VIC 3008 Australia
Email: jo-media@bigpond.net.au
or visit www.jojopublishing.com

JoJo
PUBLISHING

JoJo Publishing
Editor: Julie Athanasiou
Designer / typesetter: Chameleon Print Design
Photographer: Trish McNeill
Printed in China by Everbest Printing

National Library of Australia Cataloguing-in-Publication entry

Author:	Bragg, Alec (Alexander John), 1970-
Title:	Pants off salmon : tasty and easy recipes for impressing the pants off the opposite sex! / Alec Bragg.
Edition:	1st ed.
ISBN:	9780980619386 (pbk.)
Subjects:	Quick and easy cooking.
Dewey Number:	641.555